SIX YOUNG WOMEN PUTTING ON A PLAY

First published in 2025 by Wordville
(info@wordville.net)

Six Young Women Putting on a Play© Richard Nelson, 2025

ISBN: 9781068233401

10 9 8 7 6 5 4 3 2 1

Richard Nelson

SIX YOUNG WOMEN PUTTING ON A PLAY

A DIARY OF THEATRE AND WAR
KYIV, WINTER 2025

Foreword by John Lahr

RICHARD NELSON

RICHARD NELSON has directed over twenty of his plays, as well as those by Chekhov and Turgenev. His plays include *The Michaels, Illyria, The Gabriels* (*Hungry, What Did You Expect?* and *Women of a Certain Age*), *The Apple Family Plays* (*That Hopey Changey Thing, Sweet and Sad, Sorry* and *Regular Singing*), *Conversations in Tusculum, Nikolai and the Others, Farewell to the Theatre, An Actor Convalescing in Devon, Goodnight Children Everywhere* (Olivier Award Best Play), *Two Shakespearean Actors* (Tony Nomination, Best Play), *Some Americans Abroad* (Olivier Nomination, Best Comedy), and others. His musicals include *James Joyce's The Dead* (with Shaun Davey, Tony Award Best Book of a Musical, Tony nomination for Best Musical); his screenplays include *Hyde Park on Hudson* (Roger Michell, director). With Richard Pevear and Larissa Volokhonsky, he has co-translated plays by Chekhov, Gogol, Turgenev, and Bulgakov. He is an Honorary Associate Artist of the Royal Shakespeare Company and recipient of the PEN/Laura Pels 'Master Playwright' Award. He recently directed his play, *Notre Vie Dans l'Art* at the Théâtre du Soleil in Paris, translated by Ariane Mnouchkine. He lives in Upstate New York.

"I am more than what has happened to me."

Scene 5, *When The Hurlyburly's Done*

TABLE OF CONTENTS

FOREWORD

ON JANUARY 4, 2025, after an 18-hour train ride from Warsaw, Richard Nelson arrived in battle-scarred Kyiv to mount *When the Hurlyburly's Done* at the Theatre on Podil, a play he'd written specifically for the theatre and whose starting point was Les Kurbas's *Macbeth*, a historic 1920 production which toured the countryside bartering tickets for food, the first performance of any Shakespearean play in Ukrainian. (Kurbas, one of the greatest figures in Ukrainian cultural history and among the foremost avant-garde directors of the twentieth century, was executed in 1937, a victim of Stalin's purges.)

'My real ambition here is to write a play about a group of young women putting on a play in the middle of a [civil] war"— 1917-1921—"to be performed by a group of young women putting on this play in the middle of a war," Nelson writes in his limpid, astute Diary, *Six Young Women Putting on a Play: A Diary of Theatre and War*. He goes on: "The play was a way to talk about the war, and the war was a way to talk about the play."

Back in the day, Kurbas's production was some kind of pioneering enterprise; likewise, Nelson is some kind of theatrical pilgrim. After 50 years at his craft, stymied at home by the changing tastes of producers and paying customers, Nelson has shifted his play-making primarily from America to Europe. "I feel the American theater scene is very bleak, and utterly commercial," he said. As his Diary exemplifies, Nelson's choice to take up residence in Kyiv amidst the storm of war is not just a pragmatic decision to extend his distinguished career but a quest to recover in the doom of the Ukraine's existential uncertainty a sense of theatre's necessity and humanizing magic.

In America, where the soporific distractions of television and the social media dominate and spellbind the public, theatre has been marginalized. In Kyiv, as Nelson noted in his preface to the Ukrainian publication of *When the Hurlyburly's Done*, theatre has become crucial to the community's psychic survival. "The theatres are packed, and it seems they have become more needed than at any time in living memory."

Here, under constant drone and missile attacks Nelson's sleep-starved existence is spent shuttling from underground air-raid shelters (hunkered down sometimes twice a night, at least once for seven hours) to the rehearsal room where Nelson works to release his actors' braced, war-ravaged emotions as they explore the Ukrainian past and their present. His repeated director's mantra to his young female ensemble is "not to act, but be."

The ambition of Nelson's elegant, understated eloquence is to engineer "a profound intimacy that is deep, honest, alive, human and extraordinary to witness," he writes. To him, the show of emotion is the greatest show on earth. "These young women who have gone through a great deal have no need to show each other how sad or difficult things have been or are, they just need to have the opportunity to talk," he notes, adding, "I say this about both the characters and about my actors."

In the play, under the constant threat of terror's absurd death, the actresses cook, eat, wrangle children, dance, make plans, gossip, talk shop. Nothing happens, yet everything happens. They are making meaning and agency. They are refusing victimization. "I am more than what happened to me," one of Nelson's characters says.

Early in the Diary, as the play reveals itself to Nelson and his actors, after hearing the sound design of off-stage gunfire and explosions which is supposed to open his play, Nelson decides to cut them. "I couldn't do that here and risk triggering an audience that has gone through so much REAL gunfire, explosions, bombings. That would be insensitive and wrong."

Nelson's dramatic focus is not war's external chaos but his characters' internal resistance to it. He lets the shock of normality counter the shock of brutality. "To make something at this time is itself at least a very human undertaking," he writes.

In the play, the actresses draw together and make a space for community; in the Diary, among the six actresses, the same tendrils of connection and confidence are shown to slowly emerge. "I feel I have released them into their own thinking, letting them find their way, in ways that are rare for them, and exciting," Nelson notes, late in the process, adding, "they are solving many problems in the play on their own."

For the audience as well as the actors, problem-solving is theatre's game, both its secret pleasure and its regenerative power. Theatre brings people together; it stimulates thought. Terrorism's strategic goal is to kill thought: to make people so afraid, so demoralized, so wary of each other and of community, that in panic—to shed their stupefied confusion and anxiety—the petrified citizenry makes ill-informed decisions and the society by degrees implodes from within.

When the Hurlyburly's Done informs the heart instead of numbing it. Nelson's Diary is unique in its vivid demonstration of theatre's effectiveness as a means of anti-terrorism. "For Ukrainians now so much is about getting through the day, the play allowed one to open up and feel things and cry," Nelson reports one viewer's compliment to him.

The wallop of connection—the reciprocal swap of energy between actor and audience—is healing; it breeds courage. And courage is contagious. The Diary bears witness to this alchemy. "When the characters sing the song at the end, pounding the table and singing in defiance of what these characters will face in their lives, singing a silly Ukrainian song about dumplings, the audience joined in first clapping, stomping, then singing along with the actresses," Nelson reports to his Diary a few days after. He continues: "When it was over and the actors were leaving the stage, the audience was on its feet in one second, before anyone had left the stage, and they were not just applauding, but literally cheering and stomping. The actresses came back, they acknowledged me—and they let out a cheer—directed at me."

By the end of *Six Young Women Putting on a Play* my guess is that the reader will be cheering Nelson and his big-hearted endeavour, too. "I seem to have articulated something that people hadn't imagined could be articulated," he writes, somewhat surprised at the depth of public response to his terrific play. For the audience and himself, Nelson had worked theatre's healing magic. He had named the audience's pain and its pluck. He had held up a mirror to the Ukrainian past and reflected back its present. He had done the playwright's job.

John Lahr, 2025

Author of more than 20 theatre books and a major biographer, John Lahr is a two-time winner of the George Jean Nathan Award for Dramatic Criticism and has been a contributor to the New Yorker magazine since 1991.

INTRODUCTION

Thunder and lightning. Enter three Witches.

1st WITCH:　　When shall we three meet again
　　In thunder, lightning, or in rain?

2nd WITCH:　　When the hurlyburly's done,
　　When the battle's lost and won.

the opening of *Macbeth* (William Shakespeare)

WHEN TRANSLATING THE title of my play, *When the Hurlyburly's Done*, Yulia, the translator, asked me about the meaning of this line from *Macbeth*, as there is no obvious translation for 'hurlyburly' in Ukrainian; and, she also asked, what is meant by 'done?' Earlier Ukrainian translations of *Macbeth* simplified this line, making it into a conclusion: 'When the storm is over.' I explained that 'hurlyburly' is more than a storm, it is chaos and confusion, and 'done' is not 'over,' but rather carries the meaning of 'done for now.' For me, the Shakespeare line has no sense of finality, but rather that of a pause. The next line suggests this; there being the uncertainty of who will win and who or what will lose. Not knowing what is going to happen, while living through a pause within chaos, is the situation of the characters in my play.

The title Yulia settled on, roughly translated back to English, is *When the Storm of Evil Dies Down*.

As chronicled in my previous Diary, I spent spring 2024 in Kyiv, directing my play, *Conversations in Tusculum*, at the Theater on Podil. *Tusculum* is an older play, and much of the focus of that Diary was on my directing the play in another language, culture, and under the pressures and vicissitudes of wartime. I returned to Kyiv in January 2025, to direct a play I had written *specifically* for Theater on Podil and which would premiere there, in Ukrainian. Much of this second Diary chronicles my efforts as a playwright to create a play that would feel true to my experiences last spring in Kyiv and in many cases draw upon the stories of people I met there who were living in the midst of war, where the outcome is uncertain, but where life, even the making of theater, continues to go on.

My fascination with Les Kurbas, and my interest in writing a play about him, began on the day I visited the Kyiv Museum of Theatre and Film. From my previous Diary:

Monday, April 15th:

I just got back from the Kyiv Museum of Theatre and Film. A lot of things were not on display, but the second floor was devoted to Les Kurbas.

He was part of the Ukrainian cultural movement in the 1910s, at the time of the Russian revolution, when Ukraine tried to proclaim its own independence. The guide at the museum explained how Ukrainian theater in the Ukrainian language had essentially been banned by Tsarist Russia; productions in Ukrainian being limited to light comic shows or folk plays. The museum displays the official Russian proclamation. No serious or dramatic work in the Ukrainian language could legally be performed.

Les Kurbas was fired from his theater in Kharkiv, then the capital of Ukraine, for anti-Soviet views. Invited to stage a production of *King Lear* at the Jewish Theatre in Moscow, he started work only to be arrested, put on trial and sent to the camps.

There was an exhibit about his trial. He was sentenced to five years' hard labor, and sometime near the end of his sentence, he and other intellectuals, Ukrainians, in 1937, were taken out into a field and shot.

While in the camp, Kurbas produced plays for his fellow inmates.

Why didn't I know about him?

In 1920, Les Kurbas directed *Macbeth*; the first time that any Shakespeare play had ever been performed in Ukrainian. Oksana [the head of the theater's literary office] said this was a very big moment in the history of Ukrainian theater, in fact, it is now seen as the beginning or dawn of Ukrainian modern theater. It was performed in country villages, during a great famine. The company played schools, outdoors; bartering their performance for food.

Kurbas played Macbeth himself.

By the time I was on the train to Warsaw heading home from Kyiv last year, I had already made the decision to at least attempt to write a play about Les Kurbas and his production of *Macbeth* in 1920.

I soon began to research everything I could find in English about Kurbas, and Oksana sent me PDFs of books about Kurbas in Ukrainian that I 'translated' via DeepL, and read. Though much has been written about Kurbas' productions, his influence, and theories, the man himself remains elusive. After his murder in 1937, the Soviets wiped his name from history; it only re-emerged in the late 1950's Soviet 'thaw', when he was 'rehabilitated' as a 'good communist,' which he clearly wasn't. By 1991 with the independence of Ukraine, Kurbas, like numerous 'lost' Ukrainian historical figures, became the object of veneration and a symbol of cultural independence from Russia. There seems to be little scholarship so far focused on the complexities of the man himself. Intriguing 'hints' emerged in my research—his depression, his manic work pace—but not enough for this American to feel confident in putting a Ukrainian icon on the stage—in Ukraine.

I remembered something I wrote in my Diary, that in my experience, Kyiv was now a city of women, and of mostly quite young women.

Sunday, April 7th:

> Another observation that I've been meaning to record: on the street it seems like there are far more women here than men. More than double, if not three times as many. You see groups of women, three, four, five together. And in the theater as well; I would say that at least 60 to 70% of the audience are women, if not more. I suppose this too has to do with the war.

I recalled that when I had spoken to a group of students at a drama school, at least 70% of my audience was young women; at the masterclass I gave at Theatre on Podil, the audience was at least 80% women; I remembered looking around the theater at a performance of *Conversations in Tusculum* and seeing mostly women. I had had many fascinating talks with women while I was in Kyiv; not just in the air-raid shelter, but with students, Oksana, Yulia and others.

I began to think of my story, centered around Kurbas' 1920 production of *Macbeth*, through young women's eyes, and eventually settled on six young female characters, all but one based upon real people who had been associated with Kurbas and his *Macbeth*. I researched each of them—their children, husbands, their futures; as well as the lives of other actresses of that time.

I decided to make my play about their lives—living and working with Les Kurbas in the countryside in the midst of Civil War in 1920, *and* to make it about the lives of young women living and working today in Kyiv, where no one knows what is going to happen, when or how the war might end. So—about young women making theater, making art, during war.

When I had completed my play, I sent it off to the artistic director of Theater on Podil, Bohdan Benyuk, with this note or explanation: 'My real ambition here is to write a play about a group of young women putting on a play in the middle of a war, to be performed by a group of young women putting on this play in the middle of a war.'

My effort would be to connect a piece of essential, foundational, Ukrainian theatre history with the world of Kyiv I had found, and lived within, the previous spring. My goal would be to entwine them; drawing from my actors today for the characters of 1920, and vice versa. To learn from one about the other. I would look to connect the women I had met in Kyiv and their experiences, with six young women sitting in a kitchen in a farmhouse in the Ukrainian countryside in 1920, in the midst of Civil War. In the rehearsals I hoped to explore via the lives and experiences of my young actresses the depth and truth of what I had written about my six young characters; and via working on these characters, I hoped my young actresses would find expression for themselves.

Here are two examples of how my experiences and my play have intertwined.

From my 2024 Diary:

March 25th:
7pm:

There was another air alert a couple of hours ago. I went down to the shelter, where I was joined by a young Ukrainian woman. I'd seen her before on a few occasions in the shelter over the last two or three days. She and I were the only two people there. We smiled at each other and said hello.

And today we talked.

She lives in the Netherlands, is here visiting friends and family, and is staying at this hotel because it has a shelter... We talked tonight about the alert this morning and how it just 'suddenly' happened. The air-raid sirens went on and within seconds, there were the explosions. She said she was in a taxi on the bridge over the Dnipro, on her way to the left bank, where most of the explosions were happening at the time. She could see puffs of smoke coming up; the taxi stopped on the bridge and a military vehicle passed, unsheathing a gun which began shooting into the sky. As all this was happening, seeing her concern, the taxi driver turned around and said, "Don't worry, dear, you're with me."

From the play:

VALENTINA: Coming here, Olena. We were on a small road, in the wagons. Suddenly it felt sort of strange. The birds had stopped. I think someone even said—"the birds have stopped singing." The wind seemed to have stopped too.
We're sitting in the open back of a cart. And then—gunfire. But this is right over our heads. Soldiers on each side of the road—we're in the middle of the road—they're shooting at each other. Past us. Over us. Around us. Our driver's shirtless, shaved-head—some local, someone Les picked up. Somewhere. He sees my face, sees I'm scared. Sees Vira's holding her daughter tight to her chest. Her daughter's crying. Sees Lyuba's son holding onto her. He sees all this and the driver says: "Don't worry, dears! You're with me!"

From my previous Diary:

Thursday, April 11th:
Around 7:15 am:

I just got out of the shelter after 3½ hours down there. First the alert and then the extended critical alert. This time I wasn't alone... I was joined by two young Ukrainian women in their late 20s; they spoke English... One of the young women stretched out along some chairs with a blanket over her. The other young woman and I talked for a long time, maybe a couple of hours. I never got her name...

From her I got a better sense or understanding of the Ukrainian diaspora, caused by this war...

Both young women were from Odesa.

We talked a lot about Odesa or rather she did—about the beauty of this seaside city, where she loved growing up; about her childhood there and her teenage years. She talked about going out with friends and dancing; about the beauty of the city in spring and summer; how she and her friends would go out in a boat.

She showed me videos and photos on her phone from her time in Odesa before the war: photos of her and her friends having fun, and videos of them dancing. Her 'life before the war' displayed in front of me, there in a bomb shelter, in the middle of the night. It is what she wanted or needed to share, and I was there.

From her, I felt a profound wave of homesickness in our conversation; it was in the way she spoke of Odesa. Her grandfather had been in the Soviet navy, and had gone around the world twice and so to many places. He had told her: no matter where you go, no matter what new places you find, there is no place like where you grew up because there is something that holds you, connects you. People know you or they know people like you, so they understand you, your gestures, your thinking, and especially your sense of humor.

From my play:

> **VIRA:** A young girl came to the show this week... Maybe 18, 19. She was by herself and very scared... She talked about how much she misses Odesa. Her childhood, she said, had been there, and it had been a happy one. How special that city is—the smells, the sea. You felt how much she missed it. There was an emptiness in her, she said... She said even people who don't know you there in Odesa, they know how you think, what makes you laugh. So you are at home. Now she's not at home. And she's scared. She cried a lot...

So here is the world I would try and create: one on the page, based upon my research entwined with my experiences in Kyiv last spring, and one in rehearsal, where I would listen to my young actresses, encourage them to tell their stories and to relate them to the stories in the play; and in this way the actress and character would become one and find a profound intimacy that is deep, honest, alive, human and extraordinary to witness.

Weeks after the opening, the Ukrainian theater critic Christopher Grusha wrote about the production:

> They don't seem to be acting anything—even where the situation demands it. This is the secret of the play, because it is a special skill to be in front of the audience in a certain stage space and not to act, but simply to be. God knows how they do it. I could ask them, but I don't want to. If you're a theater critic, you'd have to figure out this secret yourself.

But this is precisely the case when you are ashamed to be a theater critic, and it is somehow indecent to write a 'review of what you see.' Because you see how these six actresses avoid the sin of publicity, and they do everything on an intimate level. For example, [Bronia, Valentina and Vira] take off their socks before dancing the dance of the three witches. And this is the moment of the mysterious secret performance when you catch yourself thinking, funny but serious, that you might have to leave the room quietly so as not to disturb the girls as they change. It seems impossible for you to brag that you saw them barefoot. Although you think you've seen everything in the theater, both barefoot and not only barefoot.

And another remarkable moment. Somewhere before the finale, you suddenly say to yourself: no, I'm not going to cry, because there was nothing that usually makes people cry in the theater. Meanwhile, your tears, which you have no control over, rise from the bottom of your soul like air bubbles from a goldfish tank.

Richard Nelson, 2025

WHEN THE HURLYBURLY'S DONE

THE CHARACTERS:

Valentina, 20, Les Kurbas' Russian wife, actress, and dancer, plays 1st Witch, choreographed the Witches' dances. She trained with Bronislava Nijinska.

Lyubov, 32, plays Lady Macbeth, has a seven-year-old son.

Vira, 27, plays the 3rd Witch, has as two-year-old daughter. Her husband is in hiding in Kyiv.

Bronia Nijinska, 32, Russian/Polish, choreographer, teacher, dancer; shared a studio in Kyiv with Les Kurbas; has two children; a one-year-old son, and nine-year-old daughter.

Maria, 25, Bronia Nijinska's rehearsal pianist, filling in as pianist for *Macbeth*; Bronia's partner.

Olena, 26, has just arrived from Kyiv to help take care of her one-year-old niece after the death of her sister in childbirth. An actress formerly with the Kurbas company. Her husband, a Ukrainian politician, is in exile.

SETTING:

A small village south of Kyiv. A room in an abandoned farmhouse. September 5th, 1920, evening.

SCENE-BY-SCENE SYNOPSIS:

PROLOGUE:
The actress playing Lyubov sets the scene and the background of the play.

SCENE 1:
The men have gone to a private performance given in their honor by a Jewish theater troupe; six women have stayed behind.

Olena has just arrived from Kyiv to take care of her one-year-old niece. The others make a meal from the proceeds of the evening performance of *Macbeth*. The dances of the Witches in the play were a mess tonight and Kurbas has asked Bronia to rehearse them before she goes back to Kyiv tomorrow.

SCENE 2:
The others tell Olena stories about the war; and Valentina's difficulties with Wanda, her mother-in-law, are discussed.

SCENE 3a:
Dinner is served, and as they eat, they learn that Olena's husband, a well-known Ukrainian politician, is in exile in Prague. They discuss emigrating.

SCENE 3b:
Kurbas has received an offer from the Red Army for protection and support; the women are concerned, even frightened, by this possibility.

SCENE 4:
Bronia rehearses Valentina (1st Witch) and Vira (3rd Witch) in the dances for *Macbeth*.

SCENE 5:

Over pie and moonshine, the women begin to talk about themselves, their worries, anxieties, losses, and fears. Bronia dances for them a work-in-progress she calls *Fear*.

SCENE 6:

Waves of loss and confusion break into their joy at being together; they talk of feeling haunted by ghosts. Together they sing a children's song, which is interrupted by:

EPILOGUE:

The actress playing Lyubov describes the futures of each of the characters and of the future murder of Les Kurbas by the Soviets on a day, October 27th, 1937 when 1,111 talented and brilliant Ukrainians will be killed, with: "each shot to celebrate the 20th anniversary of the great October Russian Revolution." She then explains: "that is all in the future. Here we are still young and we live in hope."

They all go back to singing, and finish the song.

THE DIARY

WEEK ONE:

January 1st, 2025:

Having left New York on New Year's Eve, I arrived in Warsaw on New Year's Day; actually it has just turned Monday, January 2nd as we have moved into Ukraine. On the 18-hour train ride from Warsaw to Kyiv.

My second trip to Kyiv. Before I left on Saturday, and just before I headed to the airport, I got a WhatsApp text from Oksana, who had been my sherpa, the person I was closest to on my last visit to Kyiv and the Theatre on Podil. She has been hugely influential on the play I have now written especially for this theater and for Ukraine. A very smart woman. She wrote that she wasn't going to meet my train in Kyiv, someone else will, and she might not see me at all while I was in Kyiv for the next 10 weeks. Her doctor had told her she needed to stay home and rest. So she was on "vacation," as she called it. Then she wrote, "I'm going to be a mom."

Sometimes, or often, in my experience in Kyiv, I get completely focused on my work, on making a theater production, and then something just pulls me right out and I am reminded that I am part of something that gives me a very different perspective. Here is a young woman deciding to have a baby in the midst of war.

Life. Complex and rich life constantly intervenes and gives a context for what we do.

At the Ukraine/Poland border right now. A Polish soldier just took my passport and he looked questioning when I told him I was staying for 10 weeks. I show him my invitation from the theater, so I hope that there is no problem; I'll see what he says when he comes back. As I was saying, the thought of this young woman having a baby in the midst of war is an incredible feeling. As I do and will do throughout this visit, I tie my experiences to my work, and to the play I have come here to direct and that I have written for this theater. There are six young women in the play, and three of them are young mothers, a fourth has arrived to take care of her one-year-old niece, her sister having died in childbirth. So, a surrogate mother.

The journey's been an adventure so far; the plan, as it was last time, was for me to pay the railroad company directly for my tickets, via a wire transfer from my bank at home, which I did, and then the Theater on Podil would get a copy of the tickets, which they would send to me, and I would print these out. The physical tickets would be given to the conductor in Kyiv, by the railroad company, and so he (or she as was the case here) would have the original tickets waiting for me in Warsaw on the train platform as I boarded the train. When I tried to board, the conductor said she didn't understand, she didn't speak English, and didn't seem to have any ticket for me or know anything about this transaction. Through gestures and a few words of English, I was told I could not get on the train, because a photocopy of a ticket wasn't enough, I needed a real physical ticket to board. I tried to make a little bit of a fuss, saying this is not how it had worked before, though I'm not sure I was understood. It was suggested I go back down to the ticket office, but the train was now leaving within three or four minutes. Only then did another man, who turned out to be the train manager, take me aside and whisper, '300 dollars...' The approximate cost of the ticket. So I said yes, we went onto the train, to the compartment that I had already paid for, and I gave him 300 dollars in 20-dollar bills. So I am now on the train. Whether I paid for the ticket twice because there was a confusion about the ticket or I had paid a bribe, I do not know. But this is my return entry to Ukraine. I continue to wait to see about my passport.

I WhatsApp Oksana to tell her I am on the train, and about the problem with the ticket; and that I had paid again.

While in line at the Newark Airport to get on the Lot Polish Air plane direct to Warsaw last night, the man in front of me had a small Ukraine flag and American flag sewed as badges onto his jacket. I asked him if he was going on to Kyiv and he said yes, he was. So we got to talking a little in line. But we talked much more at the Warsaw train station as he too was on this same train. We talked for a couple of hours. An interesting American, about my age; he had been a journalist, editor, columnist for The Star Ledger in New Jersey, once the best paper in the state. He's also published a couple of novels. He now teaches journalism as an adjunct at Rutgers. He's been to Kyiv a number of times since the full-scale invasion; he's an army veteran and brings tourniquets with him, instructing Ukrainian soldiers on how to apply them. He has brought hundreds, if not thousands, this time, in two huge black bags that he drags along behind him. He said in the early days of the full-scale invasion the army didn't have many tourniquets and they didn't know how to use the ones they had, and therefore many soldiers lost their lives when they could have been saved with a properly applied tourniquet and an amputation. That was our conversation in the Warsaw train station as we were waiting for this train.

We also discussed the big elephant in the room—the President-elect and what will happen with Kyiv. This is something I will follow closely over the next ten weeks with great care and greater interest and trepidation. And see how it all affects people in Ukraine, and what they think and have to say about the new President of the US.

The play I've written has six women and I am a man. The women are very young, in their 20s or very early 30s, and I am 74. It is set in Ukraine, a country I first visited only last March and at the time knew very little about. It is set around an historical event in Ukrainian theater and cultural history; something I learned about only last spring while I was in Kyiv. As I said, three of the young women are mothers, and of course I am not that either.

So this may seem a strange act of hubris on my part as a playwright, but I think or hope not. There's a character in another play of mine called *Our Life in Art (Notre Vie Dans l'Art)*, the character is the great director Stanislavsky, and he speaks to his actors explaining what we in the theater can do: "we see ourselves in others, and others in ourselves." I believe that this is the heart of theater; what theater can do, must do. Actors find their characters in themselves, and themselves in others; audiences see their lives in other people and these other people on stage as showing them about their own lives. So perhaps a 74-year-old man may be able to find six young women in himself, or they in him. This American playwright can find himself in Ukraine, and Ukraine in him.

Just got my passport back, no problem. They've been banging away on the train carriage for hours, changing the wheel gauge from European gauge to the Ukraine norm. Now I will try and get some sleep.

January 3rd.
7:37 am:

Still on the train; there is an extraordinary sunrise—the sky outside the train window is richly and dramatically red. Slept pretty well.

While writing this play for Kyiv, I really started from almost zero, because I didn't know much, if anything, about the history of the Ukrainian theater. I knew hardly anything about Les Kurbas, the father of the modern Ukrainian theater. I certainly didn't know anything about the characters I have now researched and written about.

Five of the six young women in the play are based upon real people (Bronia, Vira, Olena, Lyubov and Valentina), and the sixth (Maria) is a composite of two people. When I finished, Oksana showed the play to a few Ukrainian theater scholars to vet my work. One scholar came back with the criticism that the character of Bronia Nijinska could not have been where she is in my play, which is 60 miles south of Kyiv, in September 1920, when my play is set. He said he couldn't say what she was doing, because her diaries are in America, but she couldn't be here. It is true, her diaries are in Washington, in the Library of Congress, but her American biographer had access to these diaries, and in her book she writes that there is a two-week period in early September 1920 when Nijinska's diary is silent about where she was. The biographer speculates that she was working on some solo dances or perhaps traveling. So I wrote back explaining that she 'could' have been where I have her in my play. We just don't know.

I feel like I have researched the play well, in terms of trying not to go against what we know happened, but obviously inventing much else as well.

Benyuk had accepted the play immediately and I was asked when was the soonest I could begin rehearsals. Seeing we had to get the play translated and cast, we agreed I would start rehearsals on January 3rd and rehearse for a little more than ten weeks. As with *Tusculum*, my rehearsal days would have to work around the actors' conflicts, as they were also in other plays in the repertory. With Oksana's help, a number of actresses were videotaped, answering questions, in Ukrainian, that I had posed. These were my 'auditions.' And Yulia, my translator during rehearsals of *Tusculum*, began to translate my play.

9:12am:

Still on the train, about an hour and a half to go.

The brilliant African artist, El Anatsui, from Ghana, takes small bottle caps from liquor bottles that had come to Africa from Europe, and he strings thousands and thousands of them together in colorful patterns, making huge, kind of wavy murals that look like cloth. The very fact of them, their existence, answers the question: what is their purpose? He is making something beautiful out of something bad, that carries the stain of colonialism and oppression. Simply doing this answers the question of his art's purpose.

I think I am trying to do something similar that, where the very act of doing the play, writing the play, directing it, presenting it at this time in Kyiv, will be the answer to what is its purpose. To make something at this time is itself at least a very human undertaking. That is my answer to the questions: why am I here, what am I doing or trying to do?

12:07pm:

I am in Kyiv in my hotel, the same room as before. A lovely card greeting me, saying thanks for coming back.

At the train station I was met by the theater's managing director, his assistant, and Oksana's assistant, who speaks English. The managing director left me and went to speak to my conductor. I don't know what he said, but then he returned and watched as my conductor sheepishly gave me my 300 dollars back, rolled up in a ball. I'm told she tried to say, in English, 'I'm sorry.' Obviously Oksana had been outraged, had spoken with the managing director, who spoke with their 'friend' high up in the railroad company.

I'm in Kyiv.

2:55pm:

Our first air-raid alert; I've been here about four hours. A short one—20, 25 minutes. I was joined in the shelter by one young woman. Tables in the shelter have now been removed, and another 20 chairs have been added. I wonder if this tells a story about other air-raid alerts and so when this shelter has been packed with people. This was hardly ever the case when I was here in the spring. A clue about what has been going on during the past ten months?

I went for a walk earlier, and in front of me was a man walking briskly, in shorts, and it's a cold day. He had a prosthetic leg and he was in shorts. I think he was seeing his prosthetic leg as something he was proud of, that he wanted it to be seen, to show people, because clearly this is what he had lost in the war.

7:25pm:

First day of rehearsal. Fortunately I went to bed very early last night, woken up by an alarm at four which lasted over three hours. The same young woman was there, but she left and I was by myself. I think it was the longest I have ever been in the shelter.

Yesterday Oksana wrote me this:

> "Dear Richard, I want you to know that the train manager [who had whispered to me "300 dollars"] has been dismissed, he is going to be a conductor. And the conductor has been removed to another job, without the right to work on international trains. The managing director had asked the train company to fire both of them, but the law is not ideal. Our friend from the train company thanks you [me] for telling them. Because this should not happen."

So that's the end of that story.

I did a little work in the shelter on today's rehearsal; now I will get ready for the day.

January 4th.
7:50am:

Just got out of the shelter. The sixth air-raid alert since I got here a day and a half ago. They just keep coming. Two happened during rehearsal today and there was the three-plus-hour one last night.

Good day rehearsing, first day.

My six young actresses are each interesting, each different, and talented. They are already connecting the play to their lives and what they've been going through. I told them what I had told Benyuk when I sent him the play.

It is about a group of young actresses putting on a play in the middle of a war to be performed by a group of young actresses putting on this play in the middle of a war.

I asked how many of them, if any, had children; my Bronia has a three-year-old. She told a story about air-raid alert sirens. It seems that somehow she has gotten her phone to play, instead of a siren sound, music. And so her child isn't scared. She sings along with the alert, and gets her son to sing along with her—the music of the air raid—so he doesn't think about what is happening. I found this moving and incredible. Also I realized that having a three-year-old means that the child was born just before or just after the full-scale invasion; this war has been this child's whole life.

I handed out photos of the real people their characters are based upon. They asked if they could keep them. I notice that they put them in their scripts.

That's where we are. I couldn't be more pleased.

January 5th.
9:30am:

I woke up to the news that Richard Foreman, a wonderful and important theater artist, has died. I knew Richard, though not well; our paths crossed many times. I deeply admired his integrity; his belief that theater is not a piece of commerce but is an art. He never wavered from that during a very long and rich career in which he created extraordinary work.

No alerts last night; none for the last day and a half. So I caught up on my sleep.

For yesterday's rehearsal I had everyone. We spent 20 minutes on a Zoom with Charlotte in New York, who will be choreographing the dances in the play and teaching them via Zoom from her home. I just wanted to introduce her to the actresses, and the actresses to her.

I first met Charlotte in 2012; she was one year out of Julliard School of Dance, and had spent a year touring with a small dance company. She came to audition for a role in *A Month in the Country* that I was directing at Williamstown Theatre Festival. I don't know if she had ever been in a play before; certainly never in a professional production. I am not sure how she got the audition; and I could tell from others in the room that they thought she was very 'green.' Working with her in the audition, I felt she was special; completely truthful, honest, and open to trying anything. No doubt she had this from her dance training. Against the advice of a few others, I cast her in the role of Vera, and I thought she was wonderful; a dream to work with, and, I quickly learned, very smart. Over the years we have worked together many times, and in three of my productions she has also danced! In this play, two of the characters play witches in Les Kurbas' *Macbeth*. In this production, Valentina, Kurbas' young wife, is credited with creating the witches' dances. She had been a student of another character in my play, Bronislava (Bronia) Nijinska, who at the time of my play shared a studio in Kyiv with Kurbas, and who at age 32 had been overshadowed by her brother, the great dancer/choreographer Vaslav Nijinsky. In my play there are three dances—two witches' dances, and a third solo created and danced by Bronia herself. Charlotte and I had spent a day in New York at the Performing Arts Library at Lincoln Center, watching numerous Nijinska dances, thinking that whatever Valentina would have come up with for the witches would have been heavily influenced by her teacher. The third dance in the play is a solo by Bronia without music, called *Fear*. It is also a real dance, though one completely lost, all we know about it is from an expressionistic painting of Nijinska dancing it, and that she performed it in silence. Charlotte has created or 're-created' this dance from this painting.

My actresses have already started to connect my play to their lives and their recent experiences. Things just pop up now all the time; I'm amazed at how quickly this has happened, and how raw they are.

There's a moment in the play where the characters talk about arriving at the house where my play takes place; how it had been abandoned, with half-eaten food, a breakfast left on the table. My actresses talked about how when they returned to their apartments in Kyiv after the Russians retreated from the city in the early months of the full-scale invasion, they too found food on the table which they had left, half-eaten, in their hurry to run away as fast as they could. The memory of their returning was visceral, immediate, and strong. Just one small spark in the play opened up a quick flood of discussion and emotion, connecting the play to their loss.

1:20pm:

A short rehearsal, as some of the actors had performances in other plays. We continue to do good work.

I have lost my Bronia now for ten days as she is in another play that is going to a festival in Chile.

My young actresses started to talk about the dreams and nightmares they have begun to have working on this play.

Yesterday we talked with Charlotte about the witches in *Macbeth* and their dances, and my Vira, who is one of the witches, dreamed that she was dancing with a dead person last night. A nightmare, she said.

My Olena dreamed that she was trying to help a woman cross the border out of Ukraine and found herself in a conversation with Putin. Another nightmare.

That was last night and their dreams. Beautiful sunny day today. One alert during the short rehearsal, we continued to work in the shelter.

4:06pm:

I just remembered that yesterday we came across the moment in the play when the characters, who are of course actors, seem to be questioning themselves and why they are doing a play in the middle of a war. That clearly resonated.

WEEK TWO:

JANUARY 6th.
4:43pm:

My day off—three air raids last night—I will soon stop counting!

I did my errands: bank, grocery store, which is always a little adventure because of the language. Today the check-out lady had to help me sort out my coins to pay her. I buy yogurts, hummus, nuts, crackers for the hummus, all to have as snacks at night. I will eat all my meals at restaurants—either at the hotel or at various ones around the hotel and theater. Breakfast for me is always the same: yogurt.

I begin to work on planning the staging of the play, thinking through various options of who can be where when, etc. At the very beginning the characters are preparing their meal. I'm not a cook myself so I have been Googling recipes and trying to sort out how this could happen in the simplest way. I have done some of this already in the script, but now I have to be very specific: who is doing what, when, how, in what order, and what is needed in terms of props.

I have begun to watch a three-hour podcast of President Zelensky and an American podcaster. Interesting; Zelensky is obviously talking to our President-elect and making his case. Zelensky is a smart and clever man. He seems to be trying to reach out and make his argument in a way that Trump might understand.

January 7th.
4:26. After rehearsal:

Good day, working through the play slowly and smartly.

An interesting moment: a young woman who is a theatre student of Mr. Benyuk's has been observing every day. At some point later in the week I will let her read some of Bronia, as my Bronia is away. The student told me that she lost two and a half years of her training because she was in Germany with her boyfriend. He was in the hospital there, recovering from wounds suffered at Mariupol [which is remembered for a three-month siege by the Russians, the shelling of the state theatre where hundreds of women and children sheltered, and the near destruction of the city]. He was captured there. He had been a prisoner of war for some four months, then was part of a prisoner exchange, and was sent to Germany to recover. His knee, she said, can't bend; she mimed this. He is now back serving in the military. She stayed beside him and lived in Germany taking care of him. Now she is trying to catch up with her acting education.

I'm going to do some revisions in the script tomorrow morning. So I need to get up very early.

January 8th.
6:07am:

Spent an interesting night; three air raids. I don't think I got more than two hours sleep at a time; so it feels like looking after a newborn baby.

During the alerts (I was of course in the shelter), I spent the time revising Scene 4, the witches' dance rehearsal scene. There is some unclear writing. I always knew I would need to revise this scene once we had the dances, so I could incorporate what is going on in the dances with what could be said. I also found some of the writing was clumsy and general. I worked on this during three different air-raid alerts. And just finished.

Yesterday we worked on Scene 3b, where the characters learn that Kurbas is contemplating accepting protection and support from the Bolsheviks. Toward the end of the scene the characters talk about whether they want to have children or not, given the war. This appears to be a conversation that my young actresses are having all the time right now with their friends. My Valentina said she always thought she would have a child by age 25, she is now 24, and married, but now she has no intention of having a child any time soon.

A little before 8pm:

Long day. Talking through the play, line by line. My young actors continue to bring up their own experiences and lives. Today my Vira talked about having grown up in the east, which has been occupied by the Russians now for some time, and how she had to evacuate, then moved to another place only to have to evacuate from there, and so on until she finally ended up in Kyiv.

Yesterday she asked me to record a video for her husband who had seen *Conversations in Tusculum* and loved it. It is his birthday, so I made a happy birthday video for him.

Last night was tricky; I said I wasn't going to count air raids, but last night was hard. Went to bed early; 10 o'clock an air raid. two o'clock an air raid. 4:30 another. Each lasted a half hour to an hour.

As I left the theater today two different people said to me, they wished for me a 'silent night.' A very different meaning of that phrase than the one I grew up with.

January 9th.
5:15pm. After rehearsal:

No air-raid alerts last night and I literally slept for 11 ½ hours.

So I was ready to work and so were my young women. We could only work until two because of actor conflicts. By tomorrow we will have dug into the last scene and will have talked through, around the table, the whole play.

I met my Cicero from *Tusculum* and we talked for a while or 'tried' to talk, through mostly gestures. A wonderful actor and a generous man, he was very happy to see me. He brought me presents—a beautiful bottle of Odesa wine and a candle for my room.

I learned today that the rule allowing a theater to 'book', that is 'protect', 50% of its military age men from being taken into the army, will be rescinded for all theaters as of Feb. 28th. Theater on Podil will not be able to protect any of its actors after that date and, I learned, it doesn't know what it is going to do. The majority of its actors are of military age, and if or when they are called up to serve, no one knows what will happen to the theatre and its shows.

I also read on Telegram that starting very soon—it was voted on today—all males between the ages of 18-25, who until now have been spared from being drafted, will be subject to mandatory military training. Obviously in preparation for if they are needed in an ongoing war. So a lot of things are happening, there is a lot of uncertainty, and Trump's inauguration just around the corner only adds to it. No one knows what he is going to do.

I am off tonight to see my production of *Tusculum*; the first time since last May when I left. I will see my company after and maybe give notes if notes are needed. I reminded my translator, Yulia, that I have never seen a public performance of this production in Kyiv that wasn't interrupted by an air raid. Let's see if we make it through all of it uninterrupted tonight.

Moments later:

Something from rehearsal: we got talking about the characters as a group of women sitting together, needing to talk, for no other reason than the need to talk and the need to listen. How my actresses need to get intimate in that conversation, while knowing that perhaps there are no answers to their questions; maybe they don't even expect answers, but just need to ask the questions. My Lyubov said that after the full-scale invasion, she, her mother, nieces, her grandmother, all escaped to Poland, where this was exactly what it was like for them at night. They'd sit and talk, needing to talk, with a profound uncertainty underlying everything.

January 10th.
9:45am:

Last night I saw *Tusculum*. Wonderful shape, except for some technical things. My actors were very good, though maybe a little quiet. I am very happy; after seven months, they have really held it together, and in many interesting ways it has even grown deeper. I'm going to see it again tonight.

Benyuk dropped by just before the show, and told me he wanted to do my new play in a 150-seat theater. I was taken aback by this. I wrote Oksana later that night and she wrote back, 'nonsense, we don't do that, we don't do shows in other places.'

5:05pm.
After rehearsal and before seeing my show for the second time:

Benyuk told me he is organizing publications for both *Hurlyburly* and *Tusculum* here in Kyiv, in Ukrainian, with a book publisher he knows.

Good day of rehearsal, very moving at many different times; my Lyubov was in tears working on the last scene of the play, where the characters are intimate and vulnerable and open with each other. A wonderful group of young people.

We'll see how tonight goes; I gave some notes last night; I just talked with the sound designer so I think the technical problems will be sorted out.

January 11th.
9:35am:

About to leave for rehearsal; I began staging the play as of yesterday. I was told I couldn't have the rehearsal room either yesterday or today, but then suddenly just before rehearsal I was told I could have it, so we hurried and got some props, furniture from my other play. Usually I spend hours alone, thinking through how and where to place the furniture, but here I did it in a few minutes. We made it about halfway through the first scene. Complicated work with props as the characters are making a meal. It should seem effortless, we are certainly not at effortless yet.

A number of students, as well as some young directors, come and watch rehearsal. Today I suddenly looked around and realized that I am in a room full of 20-year-olds, so it is like a school. The line between those acting on stage and those observing can easily be blurred because all are of the same age. I must be careful; I am not their teacher, I am the director and these are professional actresses, and the others are observers. This is not a school.

Two air raids last night; one very long one nearly three hours. A little tired but it is Sunday and tomorrow is the day off.

5:50pm, after rehearsal:

We roughly staged the first scene; just where I want to be. Yulia, my translator, read the part of Bronia and was terrific.

My Vira, I learned from Yulia, had gotten upset yesterday while we were talking about the war in the play and when relating to the war today, she had started to cry. She's been asking to leave rehearsal to take phone calls from her mother. She has done this four or five times in the last few days. Now I know the reason: her mother is upset because the grandmother and a big part of the family are in the occupied territories of Eastern Ukraine and can't get out. It is very distressing to the family. I think she is trying to balance all this. I learned about her situation from my translator after she had tried to console our Vira, and while doing so had explained to me that she too has a similar situation with her father's side of the family, all are in the Donbas, the occupied part of Ukraine. So part of her family is trapped too. I assume they can make phone calls, but they can't visit, and so it is a huge weight on their family members here in Kyiv.

Every day in rehearsal another story about war finds its way in. And most every day the question of what will happen on Jan. 20th and after, is asked or hinted at to the one and only American in the room.

The visceral hatred of Russia is apparent every moment of every day. The pride and respect in a unique Ukrainian culture is everywhere alive here.

WEEK THREE:

January 14th.
About 8:30pm:

About to go to bed, a good long day of staging the play. We had four young female directors in to observe; I gather they will be with us throughout the entire process; they are on some sort of grant.

Interesting conversations on how to tell stories that are dark and tragic, while not expressing the weight of the story; how to convey, in a conversational tone, that 'this is what has happened.' A few tears during this, but I think that my actresses are beginning to find their way. They talked about how they spoke with their families, without needing to show or demonstrate that they knew these were horrible stories.

January 15th.
9am:

Just had breakfast, the same every day. Long air raid from 5:45 to 8:30; I am tired, so maybe a slow day for me.

A very good conversation with my actresses yesterday about how to tell of horrendous events; how to talk to each other without showing that they are sad. That there is a kind of need to talk about these things, and it is satisfying this need that is what telling these stories is all about. Difficult talk. But our Vira, after tearing up, found her way to do this, by not being sad, but having the need to share. I think at the end of the day this is partially what the play will be about: how these young women, who have gone through a great deal, have no need to show each other how sad or difficult things have been or are, they just need to have the opportunity to talk. I say this about both the characters and about my actresses.

While in the shelter this morning, I Googled around and I saw that Benyuk had been interviewed this week about the coming season at the theater, as well as the past year. He talked a great deal about my work with *Tusculum* and about my coming back. In essence he announced my new play. He spoke about how significant he had found my work here in Kyiv, and how important my return has been.

Trump's inauguration is around the corner; you get the sense that both Ukraine and Russia have upped their attacks. Ukraine launched its largest drone attack of the war the night before last. I think last night was Russia's response. Both are showing Trump just where they stand and how strong they are. I suspect the next few days, through the weekend, will be busy in the air and I will often be in the shelter. I wonder if by Monday, inauguration day, things will calm down.

Almost 7 in the evening:

I hit a writing wall with the opening of the play. I want the play to start in the middle of an action, but at the same time I want what is happening to be clear to the audience. I think in the morning I will be doing some rewriting.

I just had a meal with Kate, a young Ukrainian film maker who directed the film/video of *Tusculum*; first time I had met her in person, though we had communicated, even Zoomed while she worked on it. The film/video had been commissioned by the Public Theatre in New York, where it was shown last fall. It was a beautiful film that completely conveyed what I was after with my production. She told me that her mother had passed away over Christmas, and that she hadn't seen her for a few years because she had lived in occupied Crimea. There was no way she could visit without risking being arrested/captured/taken away. To know your mother is ill, and dying, and not that far away, and to be unable to reach her... She said she knows many people in the same situation. She hopes that after the 40 days of mourning, her father will consider traveling out of Crimea, maybe to Turkey, where they could meet up. Her husband is a cinematographer in the army, making army films. She talked about a particular theater director in Kyiv who has made great successes and drawn huge crowds. I realized I had seen one of his productions at Theater on Podil, which I didn't like. I found it heavy 'director's theater.'

A few minutes later:

Throughout yesterday there were major attacks on Ukraine; many missiles and many drones launched. My hours in the shelter were probably well spent. I see photos online of people in subway stations. No real damage in Kyiv that I have heard about, though in other cities they now have blackouts. Again I expect the next few days to be pretty difficult. I will head to bed early tonight.

January 16th. Morning:

No air raids. Woke up very early around 4:30, wanting to do rewrites on Scene 1. Took a shower, and went to work. Pleased with what I did. I was able to cut and paste the Ukrainian on my own. I sent it off to the stage manager to get copies. We will work on it first thing.

This is from The Kyiv Independent:

> "Just days out from the return of Donald Trump to the White House the future of Russia's war with Ukraine is dominated by a great unknown. Whether the incoming president will manage to push Moscow to stop its advance on the battlefield or perhaps he will disengage and abandon US support for Ukraine entirely. Either way, one thing is clear, the war cannot come to an end with a secure Ukraine without Europe playing a braver role."

Today the Prime Minister of Britain will visit Ukraine. His first visit as Prime Minister.

6:45pm. After rehearsal:

I have my Bronia back after 10 days away. She's absolutely fantastic and brings a whole new feeling into the room and the work. I tried to move the tables around, but my actors had their thoughts, and convinced me to return them to basically where I had had them.

My Bronia was sent recordings of some of our rehearsal conversations while she was on tour with a play at a theater festival in Chile. Today she talked about the recording of our conversation where the characters discuss having children, and where my actresses discuss this as well. My Bronia is the only one of the six who has a child; a three-year-old daughter. She was pregnant when the full-scale invasion happened; so it must have been a crazy time for her. She said if she hadn't been pregnant she wouldn't have wanted to have a child during war, but on the other hand having the child has really kept her marriage close during these times. She said that both she and her husband are very emotional, and with the child, when she cried they could cry, when she laughed they could laugh. This was interesting for the others to hear, especially because three of the characters have children and a fourth has come to take care of her infant niece. One character says in the play to another, 'you don't have children.' One of my actresses thought this was too harsh, but my Bronia, having a child, said she says this all the time to her childless girlfriends: 'you don't know what it's like.'

January 17th.
7:30am:

Woke up, took a shower, breakfast doesn't start until eight. I am thinking about this lovely hotel with very nice people. I have yet to meet another guest in the elevator, or waiting for the elevator, or in the lobby, or in the hallway. Yesterday four or five people appeared at breakfast, yet almost every other day I am alone. I don't know where these new people came from. Except for the first two days, I have always been alone in the shelter. A five-story hotel that must have at least 50 rooms. The dining room is mostly closed in the evening. They no longer have a dinner menu, they just tell me what I can get, if anything. Sometimes at night it is only the breakfast menu, which doesn't work for me as I don't eat eggs or meat. Last night the sweet woman waiting on me was very happy to point out on her phone (of course she doesn't speak English) a picture of potato pancakes, gesturing that tonight I could have that. It's an odd feeling being in a big place alone. I've been here for two weeks now. Sometimes walking down the empty hallways it feels a little like *The Shining*.

Going into this weekend before the inauguration; I feel like we're sitting on a lot of questions and anxieties.

Charlotte sent me videos of her dances for the play, which are wonderful; evocative of the period and of Bronislava Nijinska. She and her boyfriend did the dances in a dance studio and recorded them on her phone. Beginning tomorrow, she will start to teach them via Zoom.

8:30pm:

Getting ready for bed. Every night I forget about the war, then I remember as I prepare myself for air raids by setting out a change of clothes, putting my computer in my knapsack, setting my shoes out in a place where I can quickly locate them.

January 18th.
7:10am:

I just got out of the shelter; it has been quite an eventful night. Three air-raid alerts, one about an hour long and a much longer one in the middle of the night during which I could hear explosions while I was in the shelter. Again I was alone. After the second alert of two hours plus and the all-clear, I started to return to my room, and as I was walking back, there were several—four, five, six— very loud explosions that I could feel, and they felt quite near. This without any alert, so they were obviously ballistic missiles, which can arrive without warning. Whether they were hitting targets or being shot down is unclear. I turned right around and headed back down; the siren went off as I hurried down the stairs.

I've read now that the district next to Podil got hit; there was a fire, one person killed, the subway station and a McDonald's damaged; there was also flooding as a water main was hit, so water has been turned off in that area. I just checked and there is water here in the hotel.

Again strange; these explosions felt so close, yet no one else joined me in the shelter. I kept to my promise to my wife Cindy to go to the shelter each time there is an alert. Now I'm not sure if I should go back to bed or just call it a night. During the day today, I'll learn more about what actually happened.

A few minutes later:

Looking out my window, I see a truck with blinking lights, and think it is some kind of emergency service vehicle. Then as I look closer, I see it is just a garbage truck doing its garbage collection rounds. Like normal.

Just read that five people died last night in the attack.

9:30pm:

The rehearsal room has a warm feeling, unlike the atmosphere of any I have ever been in. I have six young women age 21 to 32 in the cast, I have a young translator, there are four young women who are students following the productions, all student directors, treating the production as a sort of masterclass, and another young woman, a student of Mr. Benyuk's. There is Vlad, my terrific 23-year-old stage manager. So that's 12 young women and young Vlad and myself.

Sometimes they just take off into an animated conversation with each other, obviously in Ukrainian. At one point I asked my translator what they were talking about so excitedly. She said they were talking about what they were going to wear tomorrow. Now that might seem trivial, but what I think they were doing was discussing what they would wear to rehearsal to show me, as I have told them I wanted the clothes for the show to be clothes they are comfortable in, and used to wearing.

From The Times of Ukraine this morning:

> "A man was burned alive in a car because of a Russian attack on Kyiv. After the explosions the bodies of victims were found on the street."

Headline in The Kyiv Independent:

> "Russia's attack damages Ukraine's oldest McDonald's. Opened since 1997. McDonald's confirmed the damage, its staff was able to get to a shelter in time thanks to our safety protocols, the company pledged to repair the damages and reopen."

WEEK FOUR:

January 20th.
8:30am. In America it is inauguration day:

Yesterday in rehearsal we again talked about ways a character might tell stories about terrible things that have happened to them or that they had seen. Because all of the characters have gone through so much, seen so much, heard so much, lived through deaths, murders, executions, a story that touches on such things may be told in a way that emphasizes an element that that is not terrible but rather something else, amazing or even just funny.

My Vira told a very funny story about the first months of the full-scale invasion: she was in Kyiv in her apartment. Missiles hit the building next door; she slept in a blanket in her hallway. In the midst of all this, a friend who lived a few blocks away called and invited her to have tea. She went, and given all of her fear and the horror of those days, what she remembers most vividly, she says, is how her friend's dog approached her while she was having tea, and started humping her leg. About that day, and even about the week or month, this is the event she remembers most vividly; and the story has been repeated many times. A friend of hers, a standup comic, now uses the story in her show.

This is the sort of conversation I am hoping my characters will have—not dwelling on the horror, but on life.

In the theater's lobby, its shelter, during an air-raid alert, my Bronia and I talked. The lobby was full of audiences from the two theaters, waiting out the alert, as we were from our rehearsal. My Bronia told about being pregnant when the invasion happened; how she and her husband decided to have the baby in her home town, but then that didn't feel right; so they decided, in the midst of the full-scale invasion, to drive to Kyiv. By that time the bridges over most of the rivers had been damaged to stop the Russians from advancing. They had to take a hugely circuitous and slow route, while she was nine-months pregnant; she thought she might have the baby in the car. When they got to Kyiv and the hospital, the doctor told her she was having her baby now.

I said that she was going to have stories to tell her daughter when she's older. She then told me another story about when her daughter was just a few months old; there was a missile attack, sirens went off, she was alone with the baby, and she rushed outside, headed for a shelter, when she realized she'd forgotten her daughter! She of course hurried back. I suggested, maybe that's a story she shouldn't tell her daughter.

Spent hours in rehearsal with Charlotte on WhatsApp rehearsing the dances; she's done a beautiful job and my actresses are doing great, though it is going to be a journey to make the 'rehearsal' scene work. Charlotte had put the witches' dialogue into the dances; which I think was a mistake. As she works, I take notes on how she describes the dances to my actresses; I will add some of this to the scene where Bronia gives notes to my Valentina and Vira. I have asked her to take out the dialogue and give me just the steps, from this I will cut and paste the scene with the actors. I don't think she will mind that her dances won't be shown in full, but in fragments, as the scene is a rehearsal not a performance.

1pm:

Back from the Kyiv Museum.

On our way there with the managing director, his associate, and Oksana's assistant, I learned that last night Oskana had her baby, a boy. I hadn't realized it would be so soon. I wrote her congratulations in the car and she wrote right back with a big heart. She says she's doing well.

A very sweet woman gave me a tour of a show about Kyiv during the turn of the century around Christmas time. The museum had reconstructed different period rooms: a living room with a Christmas tree, a children's room, a tailor shop, some elements of a theater—backstage with a dressing room, etc. Once again, as was the case last year whenever I visited a museum or church, my guide made a concerted effort to connect Kyiv with Europe; how Kyiv's fashion, she explained, came from France. Russia was never mentioned.

About 8:30:

Just watched President Trump's inauguration; and his speech— there was no mention of Ukraine. It seemed to be the same campaign speech that he's been giving for a long time. Very depressing.

January 21st.
7pm:

Slow day of rehearsal.

My ladies seemed distracted; my Vira was upset for some reason and needed to leave the room at one point; she was in tears. These women who are so strong, then something suddenly crosses their mind, or appears on social media, and they feel it deeply.

We got work done and Charlotte was again on WhatsApp from New York teaching the dances; she and I had a WhatsApp chat back and forth throughout the night. She made some changes to what she had been teaching. I think we're on a good track. This morning she sent her dance, called *Fear*, that my Bronia will dance. It is a beautiful work.

Just got out of the shelter, a short time there, maybe half an hour. I was talking to my wife, Cindy, on WhatsApp when the alarm went off; it obviously shocked her hearing the siren. It is loud.

I just wrote her to say that I am back in my room.

Finally we had a production meeting, props are slowly arriving, etc.—we're moving at a good pace.

January 22nd.
5:35pm. After an early rehearsal because of actor conflicts:

My young women, whom we now call the 'womans' (Vlad, my stage manager's joke) because that's how one of them explained their nearly constant laughing and joking together.

Vira started talking about the day the bridge to Crimea was damaged by Ukraine, how she walked down the street and knew what was on everyone's mind; people were smiling, people were thinking the same thing, proud of their soldier boys for damaging that symbol of Russia.

An afternoon with Charlotte from New York teaching Bronia her dance. This dance is influenced by a painting of Bronia dancing it, looking like a samurai warrior. My Bronia had watched the video in advance and had roughly already learned it.

More props arrived, rugs arrived, we are getting there; putting together our 'home'.

Had an interesting experience this evening: I had just had a late lunch/early dinner some four or five blocks from the hotel when the air-raid alert sounded, so I walked those blocks under the alarm; the first time I have been out on the street during an alert, except for the one time in a car coming back from the museum.

January 23rd.
8:30pm about to go to bed:

There's a new person at the front desk of the hotel, actually she was here last year, and she recognized me right away. She calls me Mr. Richard. She asked if I still went to the shelter. I said, yes. She replied, 'because you promised your wife.' She remembered.

January 24th.
Around 9:20am:

Every day in the Ukrainian press or Telegram chats the focus is on what Trump has said; today it is that Zelensky is no angel and he should never have allowed the war to happen. Yesterday and the day before, it was that Putin is allowing his economy to fail.

Last night when I was in the shelter, looking at Telegram, I saw a video from Moscow showing, it said, Putin's motorcade speeding to the Kremlin in the middle of the night. And asking, why?

About 3:45pm.
After a short day of rehearsal—short because of actor conflicts:

We reached Scene 3b where most of the characters learn that Les Kurbas, their leader, and other men in the company have been talking to Red Army soldiers, a wing of the Bolsheviks, who have offered to 'adopt' them as their theater company, help them with theater spaces, money, food. It is a very tempting offer because Kurbas' company is out in the countryside performing for food, without a theater. The offer even includes the chance to hold classes. But they are Bolsheviks, and the characters have seen them in action in Kyiv and other places, even witnessed a series of executions of Polish sympathizers carried out on their stage after one of their performances. So the question is: what do they do?

My six female characters haven't been asked their opinion. For them it isn't so much a question of what to do, but rather, what is going to happen? What does this mean? The scene is a series of questions and confusions that never get settled, never conclude.

My actresses today understandably see Russians as the enemy, an evil force. Cities, including where we are, Kyiv, are being bombed by the Russians all the time. My young women are angry, hurt and bitter. They have relatives trapped in occupied territories, they have friends who have died. Just the idea of joining the Russians in any way is an obvious and huge mistake in their minds (and in their lives).

However, that isn't the situation the characters in the play are in, because they do not know where things are headed. The alternatives for them are also not inviting. How do we bring these characters to life with my actresses, while still drawing from my actresses' experiences and emotions? This of course has been my effort throughout rehearsal. In other words how to get them to question and doubt, when they feel so certain?

A lot of tears today in rehearsal. At least four of my six cried as we talked about this conflict, this war. It is proving difficult if not impossible for these actresses, at this time, to open themselves up to questioning, that is, to be open and vulnerable about something or someone (a country) that they so confidently hate. The question is: how to portray characters who are lost, when in their daily lives my actresses need to feel strong and unquestioning in their beliefs and anger?

How to make this scene about confusion and questioning, asking 'what is our future?', 'what is my life?', 'where do I belong?' How to get my actresses to be open to this, when if they open themselves up to what they are feeling now about Russians, they become angry, bitter, and victims? Of course they could play the scene as victims; victims being dragged into something terrible, something they don't want to be a part of, that it is being forced upon them. But that is not my play.

In my play, Les Kurbas is adored by my characters; they love, respect, admire, look up to him. In their hearts and souls, they believe he will try and make the decision that is best for all of them, like the father of a family.

I tried to draw from my own experience to convey the sense of confusion one feels when a decision is made that one has had no say in. I talked about my youth, when my family moved a great deal, never living in the same place more than a few years. I spoke about those moments when my brother and I were being told we were going to move again to—somewhere; we didn't have any say in those decisions. We were uprooted, we were confused about where we were going, what it meant, what we were leaving, why this had to happen; but at the same time we felt curiosity, we questioned. I don't think that either my brother or I felt ourselves a victim in those decisions.

An extraordinary afternoon, where the war and the play completely co-existed as one thing, actually butting up against each other. The play was a way to talk about the war, the war a way to talk about the play. Yulia, my translator, worried that the actors were bringing too much of their own lives into the rehearsal, and that an actor should leave that outside the rehearsal room. I said that I did not want that, that's not what I'm trying to do as a playwright and as a director. I'm asking these young women to be on stage and be incredibly vulnerable, not to put on characters, but be vulnerable as living human beings, talking to each other, needing to talk and needing to listen. And for me to ask for that vulnerability, that lack of putting on a character, that lack of taking on a 'professional responsibility,' is to ask a great deal. And I know that. I am incredibly patient with their issues. More than patient, sympathetic.

I begin with an admiration for all six; their strengths, their lives, their youth. My young Maria, for example, is 21 years old; she was 17 or 18 when the full-scale invasion began. She was only 11 during the first invasion of Crimea and the surrogate war in the Donbas. They are very special people who have already led rich lives.

A little before 9:30pm:

I watched *Tusculum* tonight at the theater. It wasn't as focused as it had been the last three times I've seen it. I gave notes after —'talk to each other'. But it was still very good with excellent, surprising moments.

One memorable thing happened: a woman in one of the rows surrounding the stage left; she got up during a scene and went off to the bathroom. She came back in the next scene, during the scene, and to get to her seat she walked on stage between two actors who were talking to each other. Crossed right through, between them.

January 25th.
About 9:1am:

The confidence of a playwright:
Last night I watched *Tusculum*. Because we sort of play in the round, you can always see the audience on the other side. There was a couple who were clearly bored. He kept holding his head, they whispered, tried not to laugh. Other people were focused; and after it was over many came up and thanked me for the play. But one's vulnerability leaps to the ones who were bored, that is what stays in your mind. You start to see the play through their eyes. It's a funny balance in a playwright: because you need to be incredibly self-critical, judgmental of the work, and at the same time you need to find that confidence to go forward.

Working on a new play, there are waves of emotions one goes through as a playwright, one moment you feel fantastic that you have achieved something special, and the next you feel the opposite, that it is all a mess. I think I especially go through this because of the kind of play I am trying to write, which is one that seems effortless, and therefore 'undramatic,' and if you step back or start examining it in the middle, it can feel like there is nothing there, nothing is happening. So you need the confidence to pull yourself out of that self-doubt, to get back into it and see what you have tried to do. It's a push and a pull. Of trying to NOT make something happen. Rather to just have everything unfold organically, simply, truthfully. It is similar with actors; they want to make something work or happen; it is in their nature and training. But I am asking them to just 'be.'

We're in that place right now: one moment everything feels very positive, and the next it's 'oh my god, what are we doing?'

Morning:

Woke up this morning, after nearly two hours in the shelter last night.

Charlotte replied to the new scene and had only a few small notes, so that is good.

I woke up to an email from an old colleague, J. He had worked with me on some of my plays at the Public in New York; very smart, I liked working with him as our line producer. Though he was put into the tricky situation by the theater—of being our producer without any real authority or real power, but with a lot of responsibility. I admired how he managed, though. He ended up becoming artistic director of another theater; where either he made a mess of that theater or it was a mess that he inherited, I don't know which. That theater has essentially collapsed during his time.

During the heyday of Black Lives Matter, where other agendas besides making theater took hold of many American theaters, I reached out to J. with the idea that I would write a play with Black characters, to be paired with a Black writer's play with white characters, thereby using the theater not for ideologically or agenda-driven purposes but rather as a forum for exploring human behavior and its expression—which of course is what theater is and does. With the goal then to get a conversation going with audiences, with actors, even with those who work in theaters, and together talk about the world with its complexities and confusions and questioning.

Initially he responded with interest, then there was just radio silence.

Here he is now writing for a kind of recommendation, as he is a finalist to be artistic director for a theater I know well. I wrote him the blurb he requested, which is all he said he needed; I was honest and praised the work he did on my shows; but I found it odd that he felt he could write to me and ask for this. In my letter back I said I looked forward to continuing the conversation that we had started and that had been abruptly ended.

Moments later:

Watching the first week of the Trump administration's attack on DEI (Diversity, Equity, Inclusion programming). In one sense, Trump is right; some of this programming became extreme, had hurt a lot of people; a lot of people had been shut down because of certain efforts and pressures in the name of DEI. But that pendulum has swung to the exact opposite pole, and now any kind of questioning or consideration of diversity, which of course is important, is now denigrated, attacked, nullified, ridiculed. Diversity is essential within our country, our lives, our theater; though I think the conversations we need should be about how to define diversity. Race is but one; I think what has been missing is one on economic diversity. We now have a billionaire President who is the least likely, the least able, to address or even understand this.

4:10pm. After a short rehearsal:

We worked on Scene 3b again, where Kurbas has received the offer from the Reds. This is the choice that Kurbas ends up making—though well after my play ends; so throughout my play the decision is still up in the air. It ended up being a decision that for some time was extremely successful for Kurbas; his support of the Reds allowed him to carve out an important career and build a series of theaters and schools in Kharkiv and Kyiv over the next ten years. Hugely successful, he balanced a series of radical, brilliant revolutionary productions (using film, modernist art, stylization) with productions of Communist propaganda. Then in 1932 the Soviets fired him, in 1933 they arrested him and sent him to the camps, and in 1937 they executed him. So it was a momentous decision.

As I have written, yesterday my actors were upset, unable to play confused and questioning in the face of this Russian offer, given their understandable hatred today for all things Russian. Their characters became victims—angry victims, with minds made up.

The play isn't written that way; my characters don't know where things will go, their minds certainly are not made up; they question: is this a terrible decision? A right decision? Do we follow Kurbas if this is what he decides? My scene is a series a questions that never get answered. History will answer them, but not the play.

So how to get my actresses not to think the way they are thinking, feeling the way they are feeling, which is to confidently detest the Russians?

Today I suggested: let's assume that we are not talking about Russians, instead let's assume we are talking about Americans. And President Trump. Now what do you know, what are you sure about Trump and America today? What do you feel? Suddenly all their doubts and questioning, all the elements of the scene fell right into place. Because with America today there is hope that something good could happen, there is doubt and fear that something bad will happen. There's an ominous feeling as well as one that is hopeful. Back and forth, because nothing is settled; no one knows where it is going.

With that simple note, the scene found its footing and focus; and my actors understood. A very interesting day in the theater in Kyiv for this American.

January 26th.
About 7:50pm:

After a long day of rehearsal, working on the dance scene, which I rewrote over the past few days, and that Yulia had quickly translated. Vlad our stage manager made copies for the actresses.

Charlotte has done wonderful work with the dances, and my actors do understand that these are not dances being performed but rather rehearsed.

Stories pop out in rehearsal: my Valentina tells of sitting on the subway every day, and as an actress she looks at people and tries to imagine their lives; she sees someone reading, someone smiling to herself or looking at her phone; and almost always, she says, there is someone nearby, usually a woman, who is crying.

WEEK FIVE:

January 27th.
About 7:45am:

A couple of air raids last night, spent time in the shelter on my day off writing emails. I include one here to my old and close friend C. in England.

> Dear C.
>
> I was going to answer you in the morning, but I'm back in the shelter for the second time tonight.
>
> Rehearsals are going well I think—I adore my six young women who are full of life, and with hidden pain that pops out all the time, especially as we discuss elements of the play. Personal stories, experiences of escaping Kyiv or other cities, anxieties about family left behind in occupied areas. But we live the theme of my play—'we are more than what has happened to us.'
>
> So lots and lots of laughter, and a fair bit of tears. My friend from New York, Charlotte, has created the dances (which are wonderful) and begun teaching them via WhatsApp. Yesterday we started to put that scene together. It's a very ambitious play; and in many ways very different from others of mine, though it will look similar—a meal, a table, talk, etc.
>
> I have done little but work and try to sleep. The alerts have been frequent; much more so than last spring. Pretty much daily and often two, three, even four times a day. No one goes to the shelter in the hotel except me. So I've begun to

even watch movies on my computer as there is no one to disturb.

I am glad I am not in America right now; my friends are panicked or just completely deflated. Trump's shock and awe will not last forever, and some of his chickens will come home to roost. I'm sure of that, and then we'll see where we really are. But it's good to have this distance physically and mentally right now.

Take care, I send my love, from my home away from home, this cosy shelter.

Vlad, my stage manager, asked for last Friday and Saturday off. A good guy, I am very fortunate to have him. His best friend was getting married. His best friend was on a ten-day leave from the army where he is an officer on the front. He and his girlfriend had decided to use his leave to tie the knot.

Vlad was a 'kind of' best man, he said, running the celebration at the restaurant. He told me about a custom they have, which, given the situation where this young man is headed back to the front, has a certain weighted meaning. Vlad explained that once the guests are a little inebriated or maybe more than a little, there is a 'contest' or 'auction' where two people go around with small bags. One asks who thinks this couple's first child will be a boy; and the other asks who thinks it will be a girl. And the guests throw money into the bags, 'betting' on boy or girl.

He told me that 'boy' won by a lot.

When The Hurlyburly's Done will be published in Ukrainian in Yulia's translation. I think it is very rare for a play to be published here, especially in time for its opening. Benyuk has organized it through a friend who is a publisher. Via Yulia, I was asked to contribute this preface:

A Theater of War

The morning after our recent election, I wrote to a friend in Kyiv, where I spent much of last spring, expressing my anxieties and dismay about my country's future. She wrote right back, 'in everything bad there is something good.' This from a young woman living in the midst of war, whose home in Bucha was burned to the ground in the first days of the 'full-scale invasion.'

I am now back in Kyiv directing a play with Ukrainian actors in Ukrainian, a language I do not speak. This week in rehearsal an actress described something she had read and found interesting and no doubt personal: how in the Nazi death camps in World War II, those who were least likely to survive believed their internment would not be for long, those next likely not to survive believed their internment would last for a very long time; those most likely to survive lived every day for itself, without looking back or forward. Half of her family is now trapped in Russian-occupied eastern Ukraine; they had remained because her elderly grandmother could not travel.

My play, which I wrote for the theater here in Kyiv, is about characters who were involved in a production of *Macbeth*, which occurred in villages south of Kyiv, in the midst of Civil War and famine, with tickets bartered for food.

Today, each day, there are air raids; each day this war is present in one way, shape or another while we rehearse a play about young actresses putting on a play in the midst of war to be performed by my young actresses putting on this play in the midst of this war.

Les Kurbas initially had hoped to create a 'western' Ukrainian theater, but history had its own story-line and he directed profoundly influential productions throughout the 1920s in Soviet Ukraine. In 1932, he was fired from his theaters and schools; in 1933 arrested, tried and sentenced to the camps; on October 27th, 1937 he was taken out into a field and executed...

Last spring I spoke to a class of young Ukrainian theater students and asked about what I had already noticed: why theater in Kyiv had become so important to young people. I received two answers: because they wanted somewhere to be together and not alone, and, because of the war, they now wished to learn more about their Ukrainian culture and history, theater being an immediate vessel for that.

President Trump likes to talk about the cities 'over there' being all rubble and how Ukraine has been destroyed. But I can attest that Kyiv remains a magical and beautiful city. Its restaurants are full; so are its shops; there are crowds on its streets. And its theaters are packed and it seems that they have become more needed than at any time in living memory.

Richard Nelson
Kyiv, Winter, 2025

January 28th.
9 am. After long night in shelter. About four hours:

Tired; I was going to see a play at Theater on Podil tonight, but I think I'll cancel.

A few minutes later:

Suddenly there is a whole group of guests in the hotel; the same sort of group as last spring—older men from Norway who drive cars and trucks that they have either bought, collected, or that have been donated, from their country to Kyiv to handoff to the military here. A very good thing to be doing. This is something my friend David from England also did. So now all of a sudden there is a crowd in the dining room.

However, last night no one came to the shelter to join me. Though around 12:30 the front desk woman brought two youngish men, from Sweden I gathered, to show them the shelter. I was sitting there and they didn't say anything to me.

They were speaking English, so I could understand. They probably thought I didn't. As they were leaving, I heard one of them ask the front desk woman, 'that guy [me], what's he just scared?' That was his explanation for why I was sitting in the shelter. I find that interesting and stupid.

He also talked about how in Sweden they had given up their bomb shelters long ago and now were trying to revive them. Making the self-serving point that Sweden too feels under threat. Of course Sweden is not being bombed; Sweden is not in the middle of a war.

January 29th.
6:30am:

Got to bed very early so I got a full night's sleep before the 5:15 air-raid alert.

I have a new temporary translator. Yulia has a back issue and her doctor said she should rest for a couple of weeks. Last Friday I went to see *Tusculum* again and after the show I met with my actors. Yulia wasn't there, but a young woman working with the props was, and she speaks beautiful English, even with an American accent. I asked her to translate for me; and she did great. I suggested that she temporarily replace Yulia as my translator in rehearsals until Yulia recovers. The theatre agreed and she was moved from the prop department to help me out. She is very excited about that.

I asked her where she learned her English. She was a foreign exchange student to America for a year; in the middle of Oklahoma. She told me about joining the school's drama group and playing Tituba in Arthur Miller's *The Crucible*, a role usually played by a Black actress; but, she explained, there were no Black actresses in the drama group there, so they thought someone 'foreign' could work. Their production went to a state-wide drama festival, where people came up to her after the show asking 'how did you come up with that wonderful accent?' She answered, 'that's how I talk.' But after that she worked hard to gain her American accent.

January 30th.
8:30pm about to go to bed:

I continue to deal with the air-raid alerts, which seem to happen most often in the middle of the night now.

Rehearsal today was emotional; my Vira, while trying to give a speech about a difficult event the character had experienced just started to cry; so we stopped rehearsal. She and others went out of the room to talk to her, and help her calm down. We had touched the pain that many of them feel.

This speech is a very important moment in the play. The story she tells is about a woman they met on their journey to where they are; she came out of the woods, dirty, having been beaten, raped. She had been an opera singer before the war. While on the wagon heading down the road she began to sing from *The Barber of Seville*. Then she got off the wagon and wandered off. But before she left, she said something, which for me is the most important line in the play, a line which summarizes what the play, I think, is trying to do, to convey: 'I am more than what has happened to me.'

This is the heart of my play. This part, Scene 5, is when the characters begin to talk about the mysteries of life, their lives, how they feel not in control of things, how they have begun to recognize that they can't understand things, know things, and YET they are still not victims. BECAUSE they have ways of addressing these unsettled feelings—just as the woman on the wagon addressed it by singing—they make theater, and in particular they dance.

My Vira came up to me at a break and apologized for crying, of course I told her there is no reason to apologize at all.

January 31st.
Little after 8am:

In the shelter. Alone.

My play is set in wartime, 1920 Ukraine during its Civil War, which lasted from about 1917 to 1921; a very bloody war. My ambition was to write a play set in wartime to be performed within a country that is itself now in a war. Originally it opened with the sounds of gunfire and a few explosions in the distance. My sound designers sent me a whole set of possible sound-effect explosions to listen to. As I listened it became obvious that I couldn't do that here and risk triggering an audience that has gone through so much REAL gunfire, explosions, bombings. To put it on stage would seem insensitive and wrong. I have now rewritten the opening and taken away the sound effects of bombs, etc. The play obviously is set during wartime; there is much talk about the war; but it is one thing to talk about it, and another to try and create the effect of war offstage, when a real war is happening just outside the walls of the theater.

5:30pm:

After a shortened day of rehearsal, mostly dance; an hour with Charlotte from New York.

I spent a lot of time talking with my Valentina and my Bronia about areas in the play where I worried the writing wasn't clear; they were immensely helpful. I think they felt happy being allowed into that discussion with the writer.

A couple of days ago I was a little confused when my Vira suddenly said that her 'masterclass' had changed its schedule and so she couldn't be in rehearsal for the first few hours today. That pretty much meant that I couldn't really rehearse today. I suppose I was 'put out' because she told me this so late.

Today in rehearsal she talked about the masterclass, which was not what I thought it was. It was run by an organization that connects wounded soldiers, men and women, to the theater, to help them gain confidence, to learn to speak up, talk confidently, as they struggle during rehabilitation. The climax of the masterclass is a puppet show that the soldiers themselves perform, using their own voices. So this 'masterclass' is theater therapy for wounded soldiers. She hadn't told me that; had she told me I, of course, would not have been put out at all. That's the way it is here, you just don't know. Amazing that heroic efforts are made, and no one talks about them.

February 1st.
About 9:30am:

A long night in the shelter; first an hour around 12, then around 5:30 almost four hours.

I haven't heard yet what, if any, damage there was in Kyiv. I know Odesa was hit in the historical center of town. Poltova was hit very hard. I'll learn more. Yulia said it was a hard night for her too; she spent it in her bathroom.

Last night in the shelter I streamed on my computer an Ozu film, a great filmmaker I have long admired. I had not seen this film before, called *The Record of a Tenement Gentlemen*. It had only recently been released with English subtitles. Made just after World War II, and like all of Ozu's films, full of profound humanity. It is about a woman who is very cold, obviously angry and bitter; she finds herself taking care of a young boy, whom she first tries to push away and then slowly warms to, finding herself and her humanity in caring for him. She had thought the boy had been abandoned, but the father suddenly appears, having been searching for his son. The father and son go off together, reunited. The story ends with the woman seeking a child to adopt. In the last shots, it's pretty clear that there seem to be many children available after the war—boys just hanging around a park. A deeply moving story about healing after a war.

February 2nd.
8:30pm, just about to go to bed:

Finished the week and we finished going through the play. We've now roughly staged the entire play, and I think we are in good shape moving forward.

Arman arrives tomorrow, as my assistant director; it will be very helpful to have someone else to talk to, and to get his perspective. I first met Arman in Paris; he was an actor in the company of the Theatre du Soleil; and he played an important role in my production of my play *Notre Vie Dans l'Art* in 2023-24 at the Soleil. He is Armenian and speaks numerous languages, including Ukrainian. He came to Kyiv for several weeks last spring to assist me with *Tusculum*, and because I have been supported by friends generously paying my expenses, I was able to offer to pay his expenses and invite him to assist me again. He's a wonderful actor; an extraordinary man—generous, thoughtful and kind. My actresses will love him. There is a character that does not appear but is often mentioned in my play, the actor Favst. Early in the play Bronia talks about what she heard her eight-year-old daughter say to Favst yesterday: "I'm tired, I can't play with you anymore..." And Favst pleads: "Please, one more. Let's play one more game..."

Over Christmas, 2023, my whole family came to Paris and to the Theatre du Soleil. I remember watching Arman play and play with my 1½-year-old granddaughter, Viola. Whenever I wrote about Favst in the play, I thought of Arman.

One short air-raid alert this morning, but nothing else. Last night was great, about ten hours of sleep, catching up. Feeling very positive.

My actresses are in good shape, a little tired at times when we start, but usually focused as we get going. I feel I have released them into their own thinking, letting them find their way, in ways that are rare for them, and exciting. They are smart. They are solving many problems in the play on their own; I just tell them the problem and then they work it out. Fantastic way to work.

WEEK SIX:

February 3rd.
About 7am. Day off:

No alerts two nights in a row, so I am very rested.

Yesterday we came across some translation issues: one when Bronia talks about the book she has been writing and then how she has begun to second guess herself on the value of her book. She says, 'I thought it was going to be a pretty good book, I'm not so sure now. Or is that just me being feminine.' And she laughs.

That is a direct quote from Bronislava Nijinska's autobiography. Yulia translated it as: (this is translated back into English via DeepL) 'I thought I made a pretty good book, but now for some reason I'm not so sure anymore. Or did I just fall into overt femininity?'

We had a discussion about this; I worried that though 'falling into overt femininity' was the meaning, wasn't it too overly expressed? I learned that in Ukraine, even today, that this sort of self- questioning, about how a woman can fall into a cliché about women, is alien to the culture. Such feminist discussions have not taken hold in Ukraine. Not yet. The over-explanation of the line is actually necessary to convey its meaning.

In the play my Lyubov talks of Kurbas' execution "as one of one thousand one hundred and eleven shots that week which will end the lives of talented and brilliant Ukrainians. It will be said that each shot is to celebrate the 20th anniversary of the great October Russian Revolution." My Lyubov finds it difficult not to cry saying this. She tries to fight it. I said it is fine, fight it if you wish, but if it is an honest cry, cry.

Around 5:30:

Took a long walk through Kyiv. For three or four hours. Visited the National History Museum where I went last spring. Not much new there; and like last spring I was pretty much the only person in the museum except for the female guards who sit in the rooms. Two young workmen came out of a closed room carrying a giant, maybe seven-foot-tall, bust of Lenin. It had been in the back somewhere; this is on the third floor. They carried it past me and started to carry it down the stairs. I thought of filming this on my phone, but worried I would upset them. It was like an image out of a 1980's East European film.

Arman arrived.

February 4th.
About 9:20am:

Long night. Four plus hours in the shelter. Three hours, then all clear, then after an hour another alert for about an hour or so. A little tired.

I plan to see *Tusculum* again tonight with Arman.

On my walk yesterday I happened to be crossing St. Sophia's Square at noon and heard the church bells ringing. As I passed I could see in the arch of the entry the bell ringer ringing with both hands and feet by ropes. I had never before seen a human being bell ringer in action and I was transfixed. I noticed I was the only person standing and watching; people are used to it. A lot of priests were coming out of St. Sophia's on their way to lunch or something. They weren't paying attention either; obviously it is a daily occurrence for them. Every day at noon.

Woke up this morning to snow; the first snow since I've been here.

11:29 pm:

A brutal beginning to the night; I am in the shelter now. I went to bed a little later than normal because I saw my show tonight. This is already the second alert of the night. I am pretty sure if I actually lived here in Kyiv I wouldn't head to the shelter as often as I now do. I think, no, I could not have kept this up for three years. It's only knowing that I am here for a limited period of time that I can do this and keep my sanity.

Yulia told me that by looking at the map showing what parts of the country are under alert (I have this app on my phone too) she can tell what kind of attack is occurring, whether ballistic missiles or drones or whatever. If it is drones she goes to bed; if ballistic, she moves to her bathroom.

Today in rehearsal: my ladies were a little resistant; the first time I felt any resistance from them. I may not have been on my best form, but we started with the first scene, and I wonder if they had thought we'd gotten farther than we really had. My questioning myself and constantly making changes surprises them I think—perhaps they felt we had already settled these things.

I reassigned three small lines of Vira's to Valentina, to make things clearer—she made a comment that I thought at first was a joke: she said: was she being punished? I wonder if she actually felt that.

My Bronia was frustrated by the others who she felt were unfocused and so she said she didn't know what was going on or how to react.

My Valentina: I suggested she make a move to wash her hands; she resisted, saying she had just taken a drink of water, why would she wash her hands after drinking water. She said she would have to wash her hands first. That didn't really make sense to me.

I found myself explaining myself a lot more than usual.

We worked on my Olena's entrance over and over; nothing felt right.

So a rough day; the first rough one I have had with my young ladies. I'm not sure where it came from: from me not being decisive or clear, or from them thinking we were farther along than we are, or maybe it's just that moment when they don't quite have their lines under their belts.

February 5th.
4:47am:

I am still in the shelter. It has been a night of hell really. It began with an air-raid alert at 9:51pm, and after two more, I am still here, or here again.

I have to admit that I am beginning to question my policy of always going to the shelter and staying. I'm not sure this is right for me anymore. This is now the entire night. I have been here for 6½ hours and there is no all-clear yet. And I have rehearsal. I'd love to get two or three hours of sleep.

February 7th.
7:15am:

Air-raid alert that lasted a long time. But I left the shelter after about an hour, and went back to sleep. I kept being interrupted by repeated alert notifications, but I slept.

I think I am doing the right thing. Trying to balance this. I can't stay in the shelter all night every night, otherwise I am going to get sick.

There were explosions in Kyiv last night, I think near the train station.

Worked through Scene 2 yesterday. We will put Scenes 1 and 2 together today, and move on to Scene 3a. These are the scenes with the most complicated props—in which they make a meal, set the table, and eat the meal—so it will be good to get these under our belt.

We also have the dancing coming up, which is complicated as well. Good work with Charlotte via WhatsApp yesterday from New York.

We're about halfway through our rehearsal process now, and so at that uncertain stage of not quite off book.

Everyday what happens in Washington is big news in Kyiv. One headline: "White House bombshell for Ukraine: US aid ends." Ukraine gets a great deal of aid from the US, beyond weapons. That money is now stopped. It needs to be either replaced or those programs will be abandoned.

Mr. Kellogg, Trump's point person for Ukraine, spoke about the need for elections in Ukraine, making the same point Putin makes. He said elections can happen in a war. Well, that is very difficult when part of the country is under occupation, and the people there won't be able to vote. To have a vote without those people is asking that Kyiv accept that those people are no longer part of Ukraine and so those territories are indeed annexed by Russia.

One US program focused on sanctioning Russian oligarchs has just been ended.

So a lot of questioning here about what the hell is going on in Washington. Of course that is the question people have around the world, whether Gaza, or Canada, Mexico, Greenland, Panama; it is an unsettling time. But when in a war zone, in a war, anything that adds to one's sense of being unsettled is profoundly troubling.

People here are probably a little self-conscious about talking to me about this.

The other night in the shelter I finished Bulgakov's *The White Guard*. This was the third time I had read it, but the first time since I have visited Kyiv. Three quarters of the book takes place in the house that is directly across the cobblestone street from the theater and just around the corner from my hotel. This was the house Bulgakov had lived in as a young man. I would read the book, then in the morning stand at the window by the rehearsal room and look out at this house, see the rooms, entrance, backyard, ground floor where Bulgakov's characters lived. Amazing to read a book, and an important book, and be living right where it took place in the mind of Bulgakov.

February 8th.
7:55am. Just finished breakfast:

There was an over seven-hour air-raid alert last night, following one the day before that lasted five hours, and a couple of days before that there was another seven-hour one. This starts to appear to be a Russian strategy, to keep people like me awake.

Last night I went to the shelter for an hour and a half; I checked the various Telegram chats; I made the determination that these were drones and returned back to my bed.

I spoke with Cindy yesterday about this and she totally agrees.

If I feel there are ballistic missiles, then of course I will stay in the shelter.

Yesterday we ran Scenes 1 and 2 and it was very disappointing. After all this time they just seemed to be 'acting', and having no idea about what I was after, and so forth. Then we talked. When there are six people on stage, and they are all sort of equal, when just one moves in the wrong direction, she can drag the others there. I think that's what happened. One decided to act like crazy and the others followed, and another just seemed to be unfocused. Those two things created the aura of a mess.

I talked to them, explained again, and I spoke with the one young woman who was acting very passionately and I told her not to project but just talk, and to my amazement she was then pretty wonderful. We made a huge leap, I think—I THINK—because it is always two steps forward and one step back with this work. I'm doing my best and all I can.

When we discussed the opening where Olena has just arrived from Kyiv, where the others haven't been for a few months, my Vira talked about the early days of the full-scale invasion when she and her family had escaped to the Carpathian mountains and how they would question anyone coming from Kyiv about what it was now like, what was going on, was it safe, how the roads were, etc.

In rehearsal yesterday, we talked about the character of Olena's husband who had been a major figure in the 1917 Ukrainian independence movement—Ukraine's ambassador to the US, and had held a seat in the Duma—and who now, at the time of the play, is exiled in Prague. I explained how the other characters would have been impressed by him, he is like a hero to them. I asked my actresses who they most admire today in Ukraine, what politician? And they all seemed to say: Valerii Zaluzhnyi, Ukraine's ambassador to the UK, and the former head of the army at the beginning of the full-scale invasion. I had noticed a poll out a week ago where Zaluzhnyi polled ahead of Zelensky were elections held today, even though Zaluzhnyi has no party and has never said he was running for anything.

February 9th.
About 7:10am:

I have stopped staying in the shelter; last night I stayed about 45 minutes. Once in bed, I kept my phone on and heard the many announcements of continuing alerts, each of which woke me up, but fortunately I could keep going back to sleep. A new kind of balance right now. I check the Telegram channels for any information especially regarding ballistic missiles.

I explained all this to my cast yesterday, after they had asked me how I was doing, and their response: 'Now you are a Ukrainian!'

You want to be careful and safe; however, over three years of this makes people just ignore the alerts. So I guess they don't do that much good.

My temporary translator told me that the night before last her cat was going crazy, and she worried if the cat was trying to tell her something. She was trying to get the answers from her cat as to what was happening in the war!

My stage manager said he stepped out onto his balcony and heard the drones coming by.

Arman said he was sitting at his desk by the window, and then thought he would move to the other side of the room, away from the window.

3:45pm, after rehearsal, and lunch:

Shortened day; two of my actors had shows and my Maria is out sick for the second day.

Everyone was distracted; each actress for a different reason. My Vira was teary; my Valintina got teary, and I am not quite sure why, because this is rare for her. I think all of this had nothing to do with the show or rehearsal. For Vira, I think, it was because we started to talk about the war. My Bronia had a lot of serious questions.

WEEK SEVEN:

February 10th.
3:45pm. Day Off:

Just back from a long walk through Kyiv with Arman.

Cold but sunny; it was great to chat with Arman about rehearsals and about Kyiv, which he knows well. He reminded me that my Valentina, who yesterday seemed a little off and unfocused, had told me that she might be a little late because she was going to visit a cemetery in the morning. She hadn't been late, but she had come directly from the cemetery; whether it was a family member, someone who died in the war, a friend, I don't know.

Arman told me about a friend with whom he had dinner the night before; an artist in Kyiv, whose father is ill in another part of the country. When Arman asked why he hasn't gone to see his father, he said it was too much of a risk, because the army checks people's IDs and papers on the trains. So he can't go see his father because he doesn't want to be picked up by the army.

Arman pointed out that next to the Bulgakov House across from the theater, there's a little statue of a cat, referencing Bulgakov's *Master and Margarita*. It holds a kind of Bunsen burner and carved into it is, in Ukrainian: 'Burn Moscow, Burn.'

We stopped by Arman's favorite coffee shop because there is usually a young woman there who is very sweet. He told me about a time he was there and the air-raid siren went off. She just froze; she was tense, took deep breaths, was almost completely still for a minute, and then went back to work. He could see her working her way through her fear or anger or frustration to some sort of positive feeling.

As I was coming into the hotel today, one of the front desk ladies stopped me and said, "Mr. Nelson, are you going to the shelter?" And I said I had been, though now I don't do it all the time. 'Oh we didn't know you were going there.' I guess no one had gone for such a long while. I suppose when someone went to clean it, they must have noticed a blanket had been moved, and wondered what has been going on there. Now they know, it had been me.

February 11th.
A little before 7:30am:

Lots of air-raid-alerts.

A massive attack, they say, on Ukrainian energy. There are some outages around the country, though not here in Kyiv. I went down around midnight with the first alert, thinking I'd only stay a short while. I was surprised when two women came in and joined me.

One woman, probably in her 50s, and a young woman, maybe late 20s. The older woman spoke English; both are Ukrainian, though they live in Essex, England. They were staying here in this hotel solely because it has a shelter. They had business in Kyiv, getting paperwork done, I think, because of the death of the older woman's mother. The young woman was referred to as 'my daughter-in-law' (no name). The older woman's son (and the younger's husband) obviously stayed in the UK because coming back would put him at risk of being conscripted.

She talked basically nonstop; full of anxiety, very nervous; her husband called while we were in the shelter; he was telling her, she told me, 'get on a plane, get out of there.' I asked what she meant by a plane, as there are no flights to Ukraine. She explained that they flew from Luton Airport in London to Moldova; where they were picked up by a driver, driven to the Ukraine boarder; then crossed the border on foot, and then were picked up by another driver who drove them to Kyiv. Obviously this is much more expensive than the train; and I got a sense that she had a certain amount of wealth.

She told me she owned an apartment in Kyiv just down the street from the hotel, but as it is on the 15th floor, she didn't want to stay there. She is originally from the east, Luhansk; they left there ten years ago, though her mother initially stayed back, but eventually they got her out. She described various efforts to get out of the country, finally getting first to Germany then to the UK.

A portrait of a Ukrainian woman, very anxious, and scared about coming back. The daughter-in-law said maybe one word; her mother-in-law never stopped talking. Though the daughter-in-law did smile when I explained that I was here working in the theater.

After a half an hour, I decided to leave and just then the all-clear was sounded.

There was another alert in the night which I decided to ignore, and here it is 7:30 and the alert is still going on, after more than five or six hours.

When I first arrived and I saw all the chairs in the shelter I thought that meant that there had been some events where many people had sheltered there. But now, after what the front desk woman asked me yesterday, I realize that the shelter had become just a storage room. It tells no story. That was my imagination.

From a Telegram channel:

> "Last night Russian troops attacked Kyiv with drones and air defense forces were deployed. A kindergarten, two school buildings and a private house were damaged.

Another massive drone attack on Kyiv. The alert lasted all night."

A little after 8pm:

I'm going to bed pretty soon.

In rehearsal my young women started to really understand what I am after—just simple conversation, but with a need to talk and seriously listen to each other. And to not act, but actually talk.

This is always a journey for my actors and it will be a journey here, but today they seemed to understand and we worked through more than half of the play today. We had good talks about this; both my Vira and Bronia spoke about feeling vulnerable without being able to have an attitude. They feel they are doing nothing, and so completely open and vulnerable and I said, "yes, that's the journey. That is where we are trying to get to."

February 12th.
5:10am:

Just left the shelter, about an hour or so ago. Kyiv was hit by a series of ballistic missiles. Maybe ten, twelve. There were a lot of explosions; and you really felt them— my hotel room shook with a couple. This got me out of bed and I hurried down the stairs. I could hear more as I headed to the shelter. It was the biggest attack on Kyiv since I have been here, and that includes last spring as well.

I was joined in the shelter: one woman was already there, then came the couple I met the other day, and then a man, and finally another woman. We all sat and looked at our phones to see what was happening. There seems to be a fire in Podil [our area]; I don't know where or the extent of the damage. I will no doubt find out later.

Very sweetly, my Vira Telegrammed me: "Richard, please go to shelter." I thanked her for that. My actresses have been supportive of my not spending all night in this basement, so I think she wanted to make sure I understood this time was different and "to go."

The four women were in their pajamas and robes.

At least six different districts were attacked including the one next to Podil. One person died and I think six people were injured. There were fires and a part of Kyiv is without electricity.

February 13th.
Morning, a little before breakfast:

I have been reading the news; a long interview with Zelensky in The Economist, which had been recorded before anyone knew that Trump and Putin had spoken for 90 minutes. The fear of course is that Trump is going to make a deal without Ukraine at the table and without a security commitment for Ukraine. A number of Senators and Representatives seem outraged at comments Trump and the Secretary of Defense made about the need for Ukraine to cede territory. Talk of this being a potential "betrayal" of Ukraine. So a lot of tension in the air here; an Estonian politician is quoted saying this could go down as a dark day for Europe. "It is now clear that European leaders must take our fate into our own hands." And from the EU's top diplomat, "our priority must be strengthening Ukraine and providing robust security guarantees in any negotiation. Europe must have a central role."

Zelensky will meet with Vice President Vance later this week; Kellogg, the mediator from Trump, is arriving in Kyiv tomorrow.

Earlier this morning:

I was reading in the papers online about Trump's call with Putin. It is starting to be clear that one of the routes here is that Trump makes a deal with Putin without consideration of Zelensky and Ukraine and that deal is that the US agrees Ukraine cannot join NATO, it ends sanctions against Russia, it agrees to limit arms sales to Ukraine in exchange for Putin's agreement to a ceasefire, while keeping the battlelines where they now are. Trump would sell this as a 'win'. But it would be devastating for Ukraine.

About twenty to seven, after rehearsal:

Over the next few days I have many actor conflicts. So a tight schedule now.

Long talks at lunch with Arman and Yulia about the Trump/ Putin conversation and what that seems to bode for the West and Ukraine. It will be a sad day if Trump does what I fear he will do, which is throw Ukraine under the bus. Tragic. I think Ukraine will fight this if they are not brought to the negotiating table as an equal partner. They are strong people. They have been fighting against the odds. We'll see.

I am ashamed of my country right now.

February 14th.
9:30am:

Had breakfast, sent off Valentines to Cindy and my daughters, and my granddaughter. Read this on a Telegram chat:

> "Russia strikes Chernobyl nuclear power plant with drones carrying high explosives. According to first reports the damage to the plant is significant."

February 15th.
About 11am:

I have rehearsal later, and an interview at one with, I think, a student.

I watched Vance's speech live last night to the Munich Conference. It was outrageous, stupid, and full of half-truths and outright lies. Lecturing Europeans about democracy while at home the Trump administration is doing everything to defeat democracy in America. Incredible, and profoundly hypocritical. By all accounts these next two days in Munich will be very important for Ukraine, I will be watching closely.

February 16th.
7:15am:

A long five-hour-plus air-raid-alert last night, I just stayed in bed.

Woke up to more unsettling news: Trump aides and Russian officials are to meet next week without the Ukrainians. The headline in The New York Times worried that remarks by Vance and the Secretary of Defense are kindling concerns that the US will move away from Europe and align with Moscow. This is very disturbing and unsettling, especially as we are just a week away from the third anniversary of the full-scale invasion. It is very sad.

It feels like Trump is going to make a deal that is a victory for Russia. It is understandable that Zelensky has now called on Europe to create an army of its own. That's where we are. It's a nightmare.

Yesterday at rehearsal my Lyubov again brought up her time in Poland where she and her family had fled at the start of the full-scale invasion. She talked about how they had sat in Poland, waiting. This came up because her character has a speech about waiting, only waiting, for something to be over, then the next thing to be over, and the next. And so never settled and always at a loss.

LYUBOV: Everything I do—eat. I wait for that to be done. Try to talk with my son. Wait until that's over. Wait for rehearsal to start. Wait for that to finish. The play. Sleep. Dream. Nightmare. Wait for it all to be over. Whatever it is. Anyone else feel like that?

About 8:15pm:

A couple of days ago the air in Kyiv was very bad because of some sort of dust storm; it looked like fog but it was dust. Since then I have had a stuffy nose and slight scratchy throat and cough. I wonder if it came from that or I just have a slight cold; it seems like everyone is a little sick right now.

A few days ago I went to a costume fitting with a couple of my actors and I was taken aback because the theater was building the costumes from scratch. They did not look like what I was hoping for, which is something the actors could feel completely comfortable in, as if from their own closets—not designed and built. They were looking like 'costumes' which is exactly what I don't want. I met with the actors and we talked. They then pulled clothes from their closets—clothes they would be willing to donate to the theater—and now we have come up with something very good.

Today I suggested that maybe, to save the theater money, we would do without the pie that is eaten in every show. I thought I could change a couple of lines so it wouldn't have to be eaten, just shown. But my actresses rebelled; they were adamant; they wanted a pie and they wanted to eat the pie, as it says in the script. They said they had given their own clothes to the theater for the show, so the theater could certainly buy pies. I hadn't until then completely understood that they had actually donated their own clothes.

WEEK EIGHT:

February 17th.
Day off:

Spent the morning with Arman, doing grocery shopping for rehearsals; we need potatoes, cabbage, dumplings, apples, flour, oil, bread, and of course a pie! Arman helped me bring all this up the hill and to the theater, though I am storing the pie and the dumplings in the little fridge in my hotel room.

Last night another long air alert; and again I didn't get out of bed, though I lay there for a while listening to explosions, or more likely gun fire, as the military defense shot down the drones.

There is a concert at the theater tonight, but I have decided not to go, wanting to take it easy for the rest of the day.

This morning I wrote a preface to the Ukrainian publication of my play:

Preface

Last spring, Bohdan Benyuk invited me to Kyiv and the Theater on Podil to direct my play *Conversations in Tusculum* in Ukrainian, a language I do not speak. Yulia Sosnovska was my gifted translator in rehearsals and she is now the translator of this play, *When the Hurlyburly's Done*. I had never been to Kyiv or anywhere in Ukraine before this. During rehearsals, on my days off, Oksana Prybish, the head of the theater's Drama Department, guided me around town, taking me to museums, churches, historical sites. One such visit was to Kyiv's Museum of Theater, Film and Dance.

There, in an exhibit on the second floor, I discovered the work of Les Kurbas...

Once back home in New York State, I began to seriously research Kurbas; and read pretty much everything I could find about him in English; and with whatever I could get online in Ukrainian I used DeepL translation. I quickly learned that Kurbas is an elusive figure; and nearly all of the focus on him has been, understandably, on his art, theories, and influence. The man, at least for me, remains a mystery; and so I felt reluctant, especially as a foreigner, to put a character called 'Les Kurbas' on the stage. However, I have spent my entire life in the theater, over 50 years now, and I have spent endless days, mostly enjoyable, with actors, before and after shows, in rehearsal, waiting for rehearsal, in restaurants, bars, backstage, in their homes and in my home. And I have often written about this world. My play, *Two Shakespearean Actors*, concerns the 1849 Astor Place Theater Riot in New York City, precipitated by two different actors, one American, one English, performing the same play on the same night. Twenty-seven people died in this riot, and over 100 were wounded. My play *Farewell to the Theater* centers on the British actor, playwright, director Harley Granville Barker at a moment in his life when he thought of abandoning the theater. *Our Life in Art* is a day in the life of the Moscow Art Theater's American tour in 1923; and my *Illyria* focuses on the early days of the New York Shakespeare Festival and its founder, Joseph Papp. So *Hurlyburly*, in part, also comes from this continuing exploration of a world I love, and one that I live every day.

A third source for this play was my time in Kyiv last spring, during which I met and worked with many extraordinary people and in situations that were truly inspiring. In the theater, we often question if what we do has any real value, especially as the art itself is so fleeting—here one minute and gone the next; but in Kyiv I never doubted the importance of theater, its place in society, and even its necessity. For me this was a profound gift. I met people who told me their stories and some of these have found their way into my play. And when I sent Bohdan Benyuk the play last fall, I explained what was important about it to me: it is a play about a group of young actresses putting on a play in the middle of a war, to be performed by a group of young actresses putting on this play in the middle of a war.

Recently a friend wrote and asked how rehearsals were going and how I was. I wrote back: "The politics of the world are a mess, and my country is leading that charge. It is almost unwatchable, and certainly unbearable. But we go on. I am inspired daily by my work with my young actresses—some as young as 21, and so they have lived in war for half their lives. They laugh and they cry, and they want to make me proud of them, which they do. Our play and this war are entwined; which of course makes it all very human. And I am given such hope, every day, working with them. I am very lucky to be here in Kyiv."

R.N. Winter 2025
Kyiv

February 18th.
Just about 5:30pm, after rehearsal:

We started to work with food. We had a run of the first scene that didn't go well; so I gave notes, told them to overlap more, be excited by the arrival of the new character [Olena], and so they did. They got very silly in places and whatnot, and all of a sudden I realized the obvious—I've written a play about 20-year-old women, and I am directing 20-year-old women, and I am a 74-year-old man! So maybe, just maybe, I should try and learn FROM THEM. Watch what they instinctively do, how they act, how they are silly at times and then suddenly serious; and so I will learn from them. So that's what I've decided to do and I told them that. It's a very interesting journey for me.

When we were finishing, a siren went off, and they looked at me and I said I'm not going, then someone said it was "ballistic," and then one of my actresses said: "Richard go to the shelter." They didn't go. Just 'Richard' had to go to the shelter. They're looking after me.

Before that we had a lot of gallows humor jokes: what could we say right before the bomb hit us. When it was my turn I said I would say to them: "out of the six of you, one of you is really good. And that really good actress is..." And that's when the bomb hits.

February 19th.
A little after midnight:

I just spent an hour plus in the shelter. And may go back. My Vira had written, "are you in the shelter?" And I had written back saying I was. There were three Ukrainians with me, speaking very loudly all the time. The woman from the front desk came and got them and took them away, as if the air raid was over. I left too. But according to my Telegram chat it isn't over, so I may go back. I can hear some distant gunfire and explosions. I heard a lot of explosions earlier, when I got up and went down.

It looks like there is a massive attack all across Ukraine. This is happening at the very same time as I'm sitting in the shelter following on The New York Times live feed of Trump's press conference in Florida in which he is saying terrible things about Zelensky and Ukraine; how Zelensky's poll numbers are down to 4%, which of course is not true, it is over 50% (higher than Trump's); how America has spent far more money in Ukraine than Europe, which is also not true (Europe has spent more).

He is lying to set the groundwork for what he wants, which is a deal with Russia. So this attack feels connected to the meeting the Russians had with the Americans in Saudi Arabia earlier today in which they came to some agreements about normalizing relations. Trump made this extraordinary statement while I am in Kyiv, sitting in a shelter, under attack: he said, "if Putin wanted to destroy Kyiv, he could have done it easily. He chose not to do that." As if that were some sort of sign of a peacemaker.

The very loud and animated Ukrainians in the shelter laughed and shouted while I kept hearing "Trump" and "Americans," "Putin." A surreal night. And very sad.

February 20th.
About 6:30am:

A long air-raid alert last night, lasted maybe six or seven hours. I stayed in bed and ignored it.

Very difficult times in the news; Trump has gone after Zelensky, calling him a dictator without elections, shifting the blame for the war from Moscow to Kyiv, and according to The Times, Trump seems to be laying out the steps for withdrawing support for an ally under attack.

To sit here in Kyiv and watch and read this; and the silence of the Republicans who have supported Ukraine since the full-scale invasion began, including our Secretary of State; I guess they are just holding their breath, thinking this isn't real. But according to The Times, the vitriol at Zelensky drew gasps from both sides of the Atlantic Ocean.

Trump has now attacked Zelensky as "a modestly successful comedian who'd talked the US into spending 350 billion dollars to go into a war that couldn't be won." Which The Times called "a striking distortion of reality," given that it was Ukraine that was attacked, and the sum the US has given is about "a third of what Trump claimed." Trump has called Zelensky "an enemy" of democracy, who "refused to have elections, he is very low in Ukrainian polls. The only thing he was good at was playing Biden like a fiddle. A dictator without elections; Zelensky better move fast or he won't have a country left."

This is a nightmare.

Headline in The New York Times:

"Ukrainians stunned by Trump's comments. Fear they can no longer trust US."

The Times quotes Trump from his Mar-a-Lago estate: "you [Zelensky] should have never started it."

The Times describes how only last December Trump was trusted by a large percentage of Ukrainians. And now their rage and disappointment toward Trump is found everywhere, from the restaurants of Kyiv to the front lines, from the government to social media. People had been exhausted by the indecisiveness of Biden, and had hoped Trump would push Russia to a ceasefire. Now they are concerned and disappointed. And Trump's denigrating Mr. Zelensky seems to fall into line with Russia's public statements that Ukraine must have new elections before any negotiations take place.

The Times writes: "Ukrainians might not like their government, but they are fanatically committed to the value of freedom of choice."

A 38-year-old special operations officer went a step farther: "I can be blunt. Trump is like Putin. He will never tell the truth and makes up whatever he wants. Ukraine should not rely on Trump. Whenever soldiers here hear what he is saying, it gives them a nervous twitch."

One political analyst wrote on Facebook: "Goodbye America, we must accept the reality that we no longer have an ally on the other side of the Atlantic."

It's going to be an interesting time being here in Kyiv, given the anxieties that are here. In the play in Scene 3b, when there is the discussion of the Soviets offering to host and support the acting company of Kurbas, we had decided that instead of thinking of them as Soviets, because we all know how that ends, to think of them as 'Americans', so it would feel ambiguous, doubtful, worried, concerned, but also hopeful. It will be fascinating to see how this plays out this week with my young actresses.

9:40am, about to go to rehearsal:

Trump continues to attack Zelensky personally as a dictator and so forth. He said that Zelensky had missed a meeting with Trump's Secretary of the Treasury in Kyiv, having slept through it. Of course that's not true, there's a photo of the two of them together, talking, meeting. Trump adds lie upon lie, generating untruths and animosity. How does Zelensky survive this?

6pm, after rehearsal:

The play is coming together; ran the first half. Very pleased. My actresses are focused and they seem to understand what I want. Big jumps.

Given what's happening in the world and in my country, we had interesting conversations. Arman told me he was talking to one of our actresses, and she said, 'there still is a big difference between Russia and America, and that is—America is far away. Russia is right there.'

My Vira asked me to talk about what is happening in America and Trump. She asked, how did this happen? How was he re-elected after a first term that didn't seem to go so well? I tried to explain.

My head is very stuffy. I'm not sure if this is because of a minor cold or some pollution in the air—a kind of dust storm passing through Kyiv. I felt pretty good for most of the day, but after having a bite to eat I am stuffy again.

February 21st.
About 6:30am. Just got up:

Spent about an hour in the shelter last night. The siren went off, I ignored it, stayed in bed, fell back to sleep, then was woken by some explosions and artillery fire, shooting at the drones; that's what it said on my Telegram chat. I got dressed; and while getting ready I got a text from my Vira saying, "Richard, please go to shelter." So I did.

I was the only one there. I stayed about 45 minutes; the alarm was still on. I went back to bed. I did hear some distant explosions. But I fell asleep. I was woken up by the 'All Clear,' as I had kept my phone on next to the bed.

While in the shelter I maybe foolishly read the news, which is depressing. Is this America's betrayal of Ukraine? Is Trump's goal now to get rid of Zelensky? He continues to insult him. The urge to have elections is an effort to divide Ukraine and create political confusions, so Ukraine would become more malleable. The Europeans are struggling to figure out how to respond. They are talking about various levers of power that Trump could have not only over Ukraine and the war—not give supplies, not give arms—but also with things like Starlink, which is the satellite system the Ukrainian army uses to communicate. It is owned by Elon Musk. So America could unplug. They could basically make it so Ukraine could not fight. But Ukraine will fight, so it will be a mess, and potentially a serious situation for Ukraine and its people.

I sit in the middle of this, putting on a play; all going well in rehearsal, I adore my young actresses; we move forward.

About 6:40pm, after rehearsal:

The rehearsal ended on a somber note, when my Valentina seemed upset; I asked her what was wrong, and she said a "mate," a good friend of hers from drama school, had just been killed, he was in the army. She had only just heard this. Now she was waiting to hear about the funeral. She is a tough, strong woman; and prides herself on being that way. We carried on. We had a full day of rehearsal, but it was a little in and out of focus.

Otherwise we move forward; we temporarily lost one of our tables to another show today and we lose it again tomorrow, though we may get it back on Sunday. I asked if I could get food for a run of the play on Saturday, but was told I couldn't until after 3pm, which is too late for a run. Anyway, we aren't ready for a run tomorrow; so the plan is to have a run first thing Sunday morning.

Also yesterday at the start of rehearsal, when my Valentina told me about the death of her friend/soldier: Vlad the stage manager brought into the rehearsal room a blood pressure machine to check her blood pressure. First time I'd seen that; but it seemed like it was something they were all used to doing and had done numerous times before. A hint of what they are feeling but not showing.

The cover of Der Spiegel this week: a big photo of Zelensky and the word in yellow "Betrayed." Then in smaller letters, "First Zelensky and then us? The United States' radical abandonment of its allies."

I saw this online about my show:

"On March 7, 8, 9, the Podil Theater invites you to the premiere of the play "When the Storm of Evil Dies Down" by American playwright and director Richard Nelson, inspired by the work of Les Kurbas.

Les Kurbas is a true pride of Ukrainian theater, and the study of his work is even more necessary in today's realities. Inspired by the history of Ukrainian theater, an American, Richard Nelson, wrote his own play about our Les. Soon, the Kyiv theater audience will welcome a new breath of Kurbas's work.

What is the play about?

The audience will gradually observe a dinner that took place on September 5, 1920, in a village near Kyiv, where Kurbas's team went on tour from the war-torn and famine-stricken capital. On stage are 4 actresses, a pianist, and a choreographer who stayed behind with their children while Kurbas and the rest of the company attended a local theater performance staged in honor of their arrival.

From the everyday conversations of these women we learn about the curious moments of the performance, their lives, jokes at each other, gossip, all while being in complete uncertainty and fear for the lives of their loved ones.

The idea behind the production

"The idea of the production is to draw this subtle parallel between the circumstances in which Kurbas worked and

Ukrainians who are now continuing to create art in the midst of the Great War. My play is about actresses rehearsing their production during wartime, and the actresses who will be playing this play are also rehearsing it while in wartime Kyiv, but at the same time, feeling a strong need and joy to be together and create theater."—Richard Nelson."

It quotes from a review of my work in The New York Times:

> "With Nelson, the extraordinary is born out of the ordinary. Revelations are not in monologues, but in random remarks. And, above all, in the pursuit of truth, the characters speak to each other, not to the audience. Nelson reminds the actors: a play is not a text, but the relationships you build with each other. "

February 23rd.
About 6:30am:

Long night of air-raid alerts.

Three, starting from 10pm all the way to one o'clock going on even now. With maybe two half-hour breaks. I didn't go down until just now as I saw that missiles were being launched. I read that it was a massive drone attack, no injuries, just damage to a warehouse; the wreckage of a drone also landed in the center of Kyiv in the botanical gardens.

My Vira WhatsApped me to go to the shelter; but I didn't get that because I was asleep. So I basically slept through this one, maybe like a real Ukrainian.

I read just now online that in an interview last night, Trump said, given all he has done since his inauguration, he has now "passed" George Washington as the greatest American President ever. He found that so "amazing."

Later the same day:

We are on the cusp of the third anniversary of the full-scale invasion. We'll see what that means; I'm sure it will be eventful in some way, I'm not sure how. Maybe tomorrow with Arman I'll go to Independence Square, which has become a memorial for those who have died in the war.

I wonder how, if at all, Russia responds to this anniversary.

WEEK NINE:

February 24th.
7am. Day off:

Today marks three years since Russia's full-scale invasion of Ukraine. Two nights ago, Russia launched its largest drone attack against Ukraine since the war began.

About 5pm:

Leaders of something like 14 countries are here to show their support and solidarity to the Ukrainian government and the Ukrainian people. In America, the Secretary of Defense is pushing the G7 to remove any reference to Russia being the invader in its statement about the war to be released today.

I went to the theater this morning, to the small theater where we will be performing and realized that the way I had organized the furniture in the rehearsal room isn't quite right for this space, as there are serious sight-line issues. I've had to push furniture farther upstage. Which means the dances will be in a different part of the stage; this will require a certain amount of restaging tomorrow.

Arman and I took a leisurely walk through Kyiv; lovely sunny day, lots of people on the street. I read that there were huge traffic jams because of all the dignitaries. Leaders of EU nations as well as Prime Minister Justin Trudeau were all here.

While I was at the theater, there was an air-raid alert warning of possible ballistic missiles. It lasted about half an hour or 40 minutes. If there were any attack on Kyiv during the day today and if anyone of these dignitaries were to be hurt, that would be a serious escalation of this war.

Arman took me to a restaurant called the Veteran's Pizza, which is run by veterans of this war; all proceeds or profits go to a veterans' organization. It was decorated in a war motif; our table had a glass top through which you could see many bullets; there were all sorts of weaponry around, photos of the war, and a huge wall of patches from different divisions or units of the army.

From there we walked to Maidan or Independence Square where there is a large memorial of thousands of flags for soldiers who had died in the war. Maidan was the center for the democratic revolution in Ukraine about 10 years or so ago.

I left Arman and went to St. Michael's, one of the main cathedrals in Kyiv, where a lot of dignitaries had been earlier or were still coming; there were many cameras set up, etc. and a lot of security. I wanted to see again the wall or rather walls of photos of fallen soldiers. These stretch on for a long way. This seemed like the appropriate thing to do on this day.

I wandered slowly back to the hotel. I had had good talks with Arman who told me more about the young soldier from the drama school, my Valentina's friend, who died last week and whose funeral is now on Wednesday. The young soldier had been back in Kyiv on leave only last week to see his girlfriend and they had pictures taken together then. Arman told me how personally he himself had taken this death; Arman being an actor. He said this death touched his profession in a visceral way.

The sun is now setting out my hotel window on this Feb. 24th.

February 25th.
About 7:15, before breakfast:

Air-raids all night, one still going on. I wanted to write down a list of what comes across on the Telegram channel during these raids—here over just one hour:

5:26: Previously, 4 Tu-95 MS aircraft launched cruise missiles from the area of Engels, Saratov region. Follow our messages! In case of an air-raid alert, go to the shelter!

5:33: Attention! "Shakhty" in Sumy region heading southwest. "Shakhty" in Chernihiv region heading to Kyiv region. "Shakhty" in the center of Kyiv region heading northwest. "Shakhty" in Zhytomyr region heading west and east. "Shakhty" in the north of Vinnytsia region heading west.

5:52: Attention! Cruise missiles in Chernihiv region, southbound.

5:57: They continue to move towards the Kyiv region.

6:02: Attention! Cruise missiles have changed their direction of movement, towards Poltava region.

6:05: In the airspace of Poltava region. Pyriatyn, take cover!

6:07: Change of direction to Cherkasy region. In the direction of Cherkasy.

6:09: Cherkasy to the shelter!

6:14: The cruise missiles continued to move in the direction of Kapitanivka, Kirovohrad region.

6:17: The missiles are heading southwest.

6:18: Change of course in the direction of Kalynopil, Talne, Cherkasy region.

6:21: Another change of course of cruise missiles in the direction of Buky, Cherkasy region.

6:23: Attention! Cruise missiles in the airspace of Kyiv region, heading for Stavyshche, Bila Tserkva.

The Kyiv Independent headline:

"World rallies in Support of Ukraine."

With photos of marches in Prague, London, Madrid, Taipei, Amsterdam, Rome, Brussels, Paris, South Africa, Boston, Toronto, etc.

Also:

"The United Nations adopted Ukraine's resolution condemning Russia's invasion. Russia, Belarus and the US voted against it."

February 26th.
About 10:15am:

Last night, the front desk called me at 6pm to ask if I was going to have dinner in the dining room. I suspect I may be the only guest in the hotel at the moment, or at least the only guest who might want to eat in the restaurant. I told them I was fine. I'm sure the restaurant staff was happy to hear that and so could go home.

We are starting rehearsal later today because of the funeral for my Valentina's classmate from drama school, who was killed at the front last week. It is today at noon. So we moved rehearsal to 1pm.

We moved into the theater yesterday; I ran into a significant obstacle with the way I had arranged the furniture, first in the rehearsal room, then again in the theater on Monday when for sight-line reasons I had to move a large table back from the main seating bank. By doing that I 'squeezed' the play and made it all feel quite 'theatrical' which is the opposite of what I am after. It just didn't feel like a real place anymore. I kept changing, moving tables around until I ended up switching the entire thing around and basically kept what I had in the rehearsal room but from a different direction.

We played with that, and my actresses were very open to these changes, bless them. So I think we found our way. It wasn't easy, but good work. I think I'm pleased now.

We started work on the first few scenes. The first scene we did a number of times because one: there was the problem with the set; and two: now that we are in the theater, my actresses started 'acting' and pushing a bit. I had to remind them to pull back and just talk to each other. This is always the journey when we first get into the theater.

Otherwise we ended early because some actresses had conflicts, shows they were in, so Arman and I went down the hill. He took me to a Georgian restaurant and we had very late lunch or early dinner. And just talked.

Arman told me that Ariane Mnouchkine (the artistic director of the Theatre du Soleil in Paris and one of the foremost theater directors in the world) hopes to come to Kyiv to research the play she is working on, and while here see my play. She also has sent me her love and admiration for what I am doing here.

Oskar, the artistic director of the Public Theater in New York and a very old friend, is due a week from Saturday, so for the second and third premieres. I wait on someone from the Avignon Festival in France who said last week that she would "try" and come, which doesn't sound too much like a commitment, so I am doubtful, but also hopeful. I think this production belongs in Avignon this summer.

Air raids last night, for about five hours. I stayed in bed. I read that someone was killed by a drone in a Kyiv suburb and two or three others were injured.

I follow the news; it looks like Zelensky and Ukraine have agreed to the deal for minerals with the US/Trump. This seems to be a kind of 'shake-down' by Trump. Zelensky obviously has to keep the communication going between him and the President. Zelensky now heads to Washington on Friday to meet up in person. That is a good thing.

I start tech today at 1pm.

Last night I responded to questions from a journalist about the play and my working here:

My answers in bold.

Hello, Mr. Richard. Last year, at a masterclass at the Podil Theater, you said: "I'm not planning a play about your country yet, but I wouldn't be surprised if certain elements of the recordings find their way into my next work." Was it a surprise for you to create a whole play about Ukraine? **As you see from your question, I was already thinking about such a play, so I wasn't surprised. I learned a lot in working on *Tusculum* and I wanted to explore what I learned.**

How long did it take you to work on the play, first writing and then staging the play? **I spent a month or so thinking about whether I wanted to pursue this and another two or so months researching; then another couple of months writing. As for staging: I probably spent a month preparing, and I've been in rehearsal about two months.**

Was it more difficult to work with the Ukrainian theme? **Not difficult in the sense that I have often worked with historical subjects, but writing on a Ukrainian theme for Ukraine as an American made me anxious, even intimidated. I hope this project is seen as showing my admiration for Ukrainian culture; a culture I am learning and teaching myself more and more about.**

And which play and performance is this of yours? **I have been writing plays for over 50 years, so I long ago stopped counting.**

The press release says that you researched information about Les Kurbas from sources in different languages. In which languages and what were these sources? **I tried to read pretty much everything about Kurbas and his world that is in English; and then what I could find online or in PDFs in Ukrainian I translated via DeepL.**

Which text influenced you the most and helped you to imagine the future play? **There were a lot. A few: Irena Makaryk's *Shakespeare in the Undiscovered Bourn*; *Modernism in Kyiv*, edited by Markaryk and Viriana Tkacz; Mikhail Moskalenko's essay *The Tragedy of Les Kurbas*.**

Did you personally consult with anyone in Ukraine? **No.**

What was the most important thing you realized about Kurbas that you wanted to convey in your work? **Kurbas is not a character in my play; only six young women, four actresses, a pianist and a choreographer. I found, and maybe I'm wrong, that there isn't a great deal written about Kurbas the man; most of what is written is about his work, theories, and influence. In the prologue to my play, I have the speaker say this: "Kurbas liked to say that neither ideology nor the teaching of truth was to be found in the theater—only theatre itself." That is something I hope to convey in all my work.**

Did you read any of Kurbas's texts, were you interested in his methods or philosophy, and do you quote him in the play, as you did Cicero in the *Conversations in Tusculum*, where he was one of the characters? **I quote him occasionally but not in the same way as with Cicero, from his writing; rather** from letters, or what others remember him saying. As I state above I am interested in this view of theater as being something outside of ideology.

Why did you choose this particular storytelling format: one evening, one location, a focus on dialogues, and only six characters (by the way, the same number as in *Conversations in Tusculum*)? **The subtitle of the play is: *Conversations After A Performance of Macbeth in the Ukrainian Countryside on September 5th 1920*. So the play, like *Tusculum* and much of my most recent work, is a series of conversations. And conversations, real conversations, often take place while one is doing something else: driving a car, or having a meal. So these are conversations as a group of young women make a meal, eat the meal, and rehearse some dances from their production of *Macbeth*. I don't know why there are six characters like *Tusculum*, it just happened that way.**

And also this particular optic—to tell about Kurbas without making him the hero of the play? **We hear what others think about him—people close to him, including his young wife.**

And why this particular moment in time, September 5, 1920? **First, we know that Kurbas and his young company were in the countryside performing plays at this time including *Macbeth*. Second, this is the day before his first wedding anniversary with his wife, Valentina, who is a character in the play.**

What feedback did you receive on your previous production in Ukraine and what are your expectations for this premiere? **I was moved by the reaction to *Tusculum* by many people; and especially by the excitement they found in my actors, the way they related to each other, spoke with each other. I think they found it very 'human.' And that is what my** theater is all about, where the human being is at the center, and the reason for the play.

How many and what kind of plays have you seen in Ukraine during your stay here? **This time I have not been to the theater. Working on a new play is very exhausting—as I am not only writer but director.** *Tusculum* **was an older play so that was different, and last year I saw a few shows at Theatre on Podil. This time I have had to stay focused on my play.**

Have you formed any general impression of Ukrainian theater and what do you tell your colleagues, friends, and family back home about it? **I tell my friends what a talented group of actors I have found, a new family, I think. Generous, open, and eager to try what I suggest. It's very heartening and moving for me.**

Your plays, at least judging by *Conversations in Tusculum*, can be called not only historical and psychological, but also political. Do you follow political events, particularly in your country? **Yes.**

What do you think and how do you assess Donald Trump's rhetoric and actions? **I am ashamed by how he acts and speaks; I am embarrassed. He does not represent the country I love.**

What do your colleagues in the theater community say? **In the world I live in, which is the theater, I know of no one who voted for him, and my colleagues think the same as me.**

Do they understand our situation, do they support Ukraine and do they condemn Russia? **Yes, they support Ukraine, yes they condemn Russia. Without hesitation and unequivocally.**

"It's a story about a dictator and those who allowed him to become one," are the words you used to describe *Conversations in Tusculum*. You also explained the context of the play's appearance by saying that "there was a mood in the United States at the time that wanted to explore one of the most famous dictators." What did you mean then and what is your mood now? **The play was written at a dark time in contemporary American history: our invasion of Iraq, based upon lies. As for now: Theatre on Podil's production was filmed, supported by the Public Theater in New York. One week after Trump's election, the film was shown at the Public Theater for an audience of about 300, with English subtitles. The woman next to me wept through half of it. For many in that audience it was about Trump.**

Can you imagine a play with a similar description, but which would be about the United States today? **Yes. As I just said.**

February 27th.
4:31am:

In the shelter; the alarms had gone on for quite a while, but I was sleeping, then I was woken up by sounds of explosions and gunfire not that far away. I hurriedly got dressed and came down here. I am the only one here.

I was half dreaming about my play. No surprise there.

Rehearsals yesterday were difficult and somewhat frustrating; my young ladies are getting tense, anxious about the show; they are young, and so have less history, experience to fall back on. This is a very new experience for them, so it is hard.

One came to rehearsal directly from the funeral of her friend; she had been crying just before rehearsal. Another seemed to have a bad headache or aches, she was covering her head and eyes at certain times. Another's kid is getting over the flu and so she hadn't slept. A fourth was distracted by her phone—I was told that she has a friend at the front so she keeps checking what's going on. And I'm restaging as I go along because of the reconfiguration of the furniture, so it's difficult.

So right in the midst of my dreaming about rehearsals, I'm woken up by explosions, which of course puts it all in perspective. We are in the middle of a war. And I'm just trying to put on a play; and the mere fact of putting on a play at this time is in large part why I'm here. I need to always remind myself of that.

Still the same morning:

I was about to go to rehearsal, when I remembered something from yesterday that Arman had said. We were joking about our young actresses and how tough they are. Last week in rehearsal Arman had suggested we cut a few lines and my ladies fought ferociously back against this; and they were right, there was a reason for these lines, we just weren't doing them right. Arman said, "seeing how they fought to keep the lines, now I see how they can resist the Russians."

About 6:45pm, after rehearsal:

It was the opposite of yesterday; a very good day, my actresses were completely focused; we worked through the second half of the play, and then we ran this half. It was fantastic. They do know what I want, they do know how to do it. Yesterday hopefully was an anomaly; we'll see. Very proud of them and told them so.

One interesting moment: my Valentina is having trouble with one line late in the play when her character says, "two years ago I was in Russia." That's true for the character, but the actress, Arman thinks, is having a hard time saying those words, without adding anger to them. So he suggested we just change to "two years ago I was with my father [who was in Russia]." I will suggest that to her tomorrow.

I had an idea for doing the poster/graphic for the show: to have the six actresses pose together with Arman in the middle in a copy of a famous photo of Les Kurbas with his actors around the time of my play. Then via photoshop to remove Arman and put in Kurbas; and also make it look like an old black and white photo. We'll see how it comes out. We spent the first half hour of the day taking this photograph.

February 28th.
A little before 8, just before breakfast:

As I was going to bed I was struck by a migraine headache. This is something that has plagued me in the winter months for the past few years, especially in February. I think it is due to dehydration because of the dry heat. So I took some Tylenol, which didn't help, but eventually it went away. But it was painful. I'm thinking of keeping the window open at night. I don't have any bowls for water, but I'll see what I can do. I was taken aback by this.

Otherwise one alert. I didn't go to the shelter, and slept through it.

This morning we plan to do our first run-through of the play and I look forward to that.

And President Zelensky is in Washington to meet with Trump.

About 9pm:

I have just been watching live on my computer the catastrophe in Washington between Zelensky and Trump. Trump and Vance berating Zelensky; attacking him in front of the press. This is unimaginable. The relationship between the two countries seems to have collapsed in five minutes. The mineral agreement is not signed, Zelensky tried to stand up for himself, as I think he should, to the bullying of Trump and Vance. Was this an organized trap or ambush, or something that just happened spontaneously? My guess is that it was an ambush. I guess this is just Trump negotiating in a hard-nose real estate way, screaming at people to try and intimidate. But when you are talking about countries, you are talking about war.

It's unbelievable tonight.

I'll wake up in the morning and see that the war in Ukraine is going to be very different; and I'll see what people here are saying; I'm sure they are in shock and very upset.

Good day of rehearsal. We had our first run-through which went quite well, so I think we are going to be ready.

March 1st.
3:15am:

Woke up and am having trouble getting back to sleep, given everything that has happened yesterday in Washington.

It seems to have been—and I will read others' opinions this morning—an ambush by Trump, with Vance as his partner. The goal: to make Zelensky the problem, so the next wave of argument is going to be that Zelensky alone stands in the way of peace. And so Zelensky must go, and there must be elections in Ukraine, in the middle of a war. This has been Putin's first goal in this process. Why Trump is doing Putin's bidding is incomprehensible, but it is clear if elections could happen, that Putin must feel that he could sow enough confusion within Ukraine that the opposition to him would be considerably lessened if not defeated.

A really dark day.

I woke up and saw a message from one of my actresses who is upset. I will write her later and say I am sorry and I am ashamed of my country, and try to convey that this is really not America, not the America I know.

I hope that others will see what happened in clarity and not just grab onto the story that Zelensky is the problem.

I hope that France and England and Canada, Australia, Japan, Taiwan especially, Germany, Poland all see that the same thing could happen to them. That this man, Trump, could turn on them and alienate them; make any of them the story, the one standing in the way of whatever Trump is after.

I woke up out of a dream. I think it is a complicated dream and relates to all of this. A truck comes to my house and dumps a pile of dry leaves next to my wooden house. Five feet from my house. They are going to set it on fire, to burn the leaves. But that's very dangerous. I see the mayor has come to light the fire, but the mayor is also a policeman. I tell the mayor, you can't light a fire right here; one, it's illegal to burn leaves, and two, it's five feet from my wooden house. He says he is going to do it, that 'it's what we're doing.' I say, 'you are also a policeman, I want you, Mr. Policeman, to stop the Mayor,' who is the same man. There is confusion and that's when I woke up.

I'm sure today will involve a lot of conversation about what happened in Washington. I'm curious where it will go. I'm sure there's anger.

8:50am:

I am on my way to rehearsal. I will read to them emails from my friends in America and England about their reactions to Trump and Zelensky. I head to rehearsal wondering how everyone will be. I know they don't blame me as an American, but I do feel ashamed. As a friend wrote, I haven't been so ashamed of my country since the VietNam war.

I projected my worries and anxieties on the waiter this morning at the hotel's restaurant. Usually I say thank you, and he says thank you back in Ukrainian; he did that, but when saying it he didn't look at me. I'm not even sure if he normally looks at me, but this time I gave it meaning, as if he couldn't look me in the eye. I'm sure that's not true, but that is where my head is.

Last night from my friend, the actor, J:

Richard;
Don't know if you're still in Kyiv. If so just want to send some love and support to you and those you're working with as this nightmare of our current administration grows darker and darker, particularly with respect to the people of Ukraine. Can't imagine what the mood is now in Ukraine after today's unspeakable, thuggish White House ambush of Ukraine's president by people whose names I can't bear to even write. I hope you and those around you are well

and safe. No need to reply. Perhaps writing and sending this is as much for me as for you and your co-workers. This need to express my grief at what is happening in the U.S. which of course pales compared to what is happening to the good people of Ukraine. It makes me weep.

Love, and again no reply necessary. Hope to see you soon. Be well. Stay safe. Keep the faith you have in art. Rarely in my lifetime has it been as necessary as it is now.

From my friend R:

I just feel deep political shock, as if watching a repeat of the non-aggression pact between Hitler and Stalin, with similar results to come.

From C. in England:

I am sending you a big hug of solidarity to pass on to you and your Ukrainian colleagues. We must all thank them profoundly for their huge courage and spirit defending the very fringe of precious fragile Europe.

About 7pm, after rehearsal:

It was a beautiful rehearsal. My six actresses are very strong.

We started the day with my talking about what happened in Washington and how ashamed I am of my country. They were incredibly supportive. They said they had lived through a president who was completely corrupt and so knew what it was like to just be ashamed of what the government was doing. One said, "you know two years ago I was afraid, now I'm not afraid." That was my Bronia who had a child born one month after the full-scale invasion. They were warm, before the run-through, my Vira came to me and whispered, "you heal our soul." I was almost in tears.

We talked, I read them emails and texts I had received from supporters in the States and England and they were moved by that.

It's still unimaginable what occurred. Horrific. It goes against everything that one believes about America. It turns America into a kind of gangster land. An America that a young Brecht imagined in his early plays without ever having visited. Where power is everything; power that demands money via shakedowns. Power that believes in nothing except itself. Where one is forced to constantly bend the knee.

Lindsay Graham [a senior Republican Senator] was an extraordinary example of that on Friday. He has been a very strong supporter of Ukraine and Zelensky. He has come to Ukraine many times. I believe it was probably Graham's suggestion that the mineral deal between the two countries was first brought up; he was trying to make a connect between Zelensky and the transactional Trump. The moment things blew up on Friday, Graham was outside the White House telling reporters that Zelensky must go. That Zelensky doesn't want peace. Zelensky is the problem. He was trying to save his ass in front of Trump, having suggested the mineral deal which also had blown up.

America is seen now by its allies as but a shadow of its potential and promise. It has no guiding beliefs except money. Trump is creating a five-million-dollar Gold Card for foreigners to buy their way to a Green Card and, more dangerously, a track to citizenship. When asked if this included Russian oligarchs, he said, "why not? Some of them are nice people." What this of course means is many more very rich foreign people could become citizens, and as citizens they could spend any amount they wish on US elections. Foreigners can't.

So many things look bleak in the way my country is now headed. We look for those people, and groups, to stand up and fight right now. I'm only hoping and assuming that protests are being planned; and a rich and vivid response is being organized.

That's my prayer for tonight.

Moments later:

A very good rehearsal, very good dress rehearsal.

I wrote the Avignon Festival, making the case why this play with these actors should be seen in Avignon this summer, given all that happened yesterday in Washington.

> What I'm about to ask is probably not possible, I understand. But I thought I need to ask.
>
> After what happened in Washington yesterday, getting my play and production (and six young Ukrainian actresses) to be seen out of Ukraine seems important. Though perhaps only to me? I don't know. But a play about the heart of Ukrainian theatrical culture, by an American, performed in Ukrainian by brilliant young Ukrainian actresses, some of whom have lived half their lives in wartime, about the richness of Ukrainian culture amidst the danger of Russian usurpation, seems very important to me right now.
>
> Is there any chance of presenting this play this summer? If so, is there anything I can do to get you or someone you trust to see it next week? I can even get someone to film it—though it will be unedited, and one camera from a distance—so a sort or archival tape. Let me know and I will do all I can.
>
> It is a very inexpensive production; just furniture and props— the furniture can even be from the Theater du Soleil's production of my play which they have in storage. And needs only a small space.

If this is not possible, I totally understand, but I hope you understand why I feel I need to ask.

From Kyiv which has been shaken to the quick.

March 2nd.
A little before 8am, before breakfast:

I got up early, around 5:30, answered emails from a number of people who asked me how I was and how people here now were.

In the papers the Europeans support for Zelensky is huge. We'll see where this all goes. My gut tells me that Trump overstepped. His narcissism just got the best of him, and I'm now thinking it wasn't an ambush in the Oval Office, that it was something that just occurred. Then again it might be a little of both; Trump and Vance might have talked beforehand that if Zelensky wasn't bending the knee enough, they would rough him up in public. It's such a strange time.

I've written to my friends that thank god my colleagues don't blame me for Trump.

We'll have a third run/dress today and with food. We're doing very well, and continue with another dress tomorrow, then another for students on Tuesday, an invited dress on Wednesday, then a photo dress and a press performance on Thursday, then three premieres, Friday, Saturday, and Sunday.

WEEK TEN:

March 3rd.
A little before 7am:

Slept through the night, there were a couple of air-raid alerts, but I didn't go. They woke me up, but I went back to sleep.

Yesterday in rehearsal was complicated. We had a run that was unfocused, which surprised me after the very good run the day before. I think they were tired; my Lyuba was a little sick or just tired, I'm not sure.

There was some tension; the first I have noticed between my actresses. I brought everybody together to talk about this, to see what was wrong. Because I don't know Ukrainian I don't know what everyone is saying all the time, that is, if anyone is adding extra lines or words. I learned that lines were being snuck in. I went through the script with them, asking what if anything is being added here and there, and why. There aren't many. Some were fine, they helped keep a character in the conversation; but a couple of others slightly changed the meaning of what was being said; and one or two were little added jokes. This is what bothered one of my actresses, because she now worried whether she could trust the others, if they were going to add little jokes. Were they 'in' the play or were they making jokes. She was upset.

She made her case and maybe upset another actress who was involved in these additions. We talked it out. What could work and couldn't and why. I think we resolved it. Again we went through the whole script—my asking if they needed me to write any new lines, to help a moment, etc. I think we got it all clear.

What I realized again, is that these are young actresses; some are just out of school, and so there's that element of being in school where you want to entertain your fellow schoolmates. I saw this when I taught at Yale. I think this is a remnant of that. So in our process of making this production, I am watching these young women grow past that, and leave it behind.

I'll find out how we are today; there was some worry that the tension would continue, but I hope that is not the case. I will do everything I can this week to make sure that it is not. I was very happy to have the conversation, to have any and all 'concerns' discussed and out in the open. I realized this was getting in the way of what I'm trying to create, which is complete trust in each other, as opposed to relying on yourself to get through a performance, which is often how it is with most shows.

I continue to get messages from the States about Friday.

Zelensky was in England yesterday, at a meeting of European nations announcing their full and complete support for him; he met with the King. It was good to see that kind of support. The question now is: can Europe step up?

To actors at the Theatre du Soleil in Paris where I directed my play *Notre Vie Dans l'Art*, and with whom I have stayed in close contact:

> I thought I would just let you know that Arman and I are safe in Kyiv; and no one here blames me for Trump. Last Friday was unspeakable, horrific and profoundly shameful. I never felt such shame for my country.

> The next day at rehearsal I gathered my young actresses around the table (our set!) to talk about my feelings, to learn theirs and to read to them the outpouring I received from friends in America in their support for Ukraine and their fury at Trump. My actresses were consoling—they said they too had lived at one time under a corrupt President,

so they understood the feeling. And one said to me, "two years ago I was afraid, I am no longer afraid." And she was 8-months pregnant when the full-scale invasion happened, gave birth in Kyiv during the intense bombings, and now has a three-year-old daughter. "I am no longer afraid." They are strong women and of course an inspiration.

I know over these past few days it has been easier for me to be in Kyiv than it has been for my friends to be home in the States.

So that's pretty much all I wanted to say, because I am sure you have wondered and worried about how things are here.

We have our first invited dress rehearsal tomorrow with a group of students, and we premiere the play over the weekend.

I also wanted to send you this little video. I happened to walk through St. Sophia's Square on my day off at noon— as the bells were ringing, and then I saw in the archway— the bell ringer, using both hands and feet. I found this deeply moving and very beautiful.

I send my love from beautiful, magical Kyiv.

From the actors of the Soleil:

Thanks for your words Richard !

Of course, can't stop thinking about you after this unbelievable event in Oval Room …

Unbelievable but true!

How powerful are the words of this young mother "I am no longer afraid"….

Maybe what will save the world is exactly that: everyday one more human being who will not be longer afraid…

Like Toomaj Salehi the Iranian Rapper,

Like thousands women-heroes.

One thing is sure, the Americans who are ashamed to have Trump as president can be so proud to have Richard Nelson as citizen !!!

Dear Richard,

We are going to wake up from this nightmare all together !!!

For the moment let us be "ensemble" as we are…as a big family !!

Big hug from Paris.

To my Ukrainian sisters that I wait to see very soon.

Break a leg !!!

And from an American actor:

Dear Richard,

Thank you for your message. Thank you for giving us news that, despite Trump's betrayal and madness, is full of hope. Thank you for showing the courage of your actresses. Thank you also for the bell ringer of Saint Sophia, he is an example to follow. For Kyiv, for Ukraine, for Europe, we must ring the tocsin.

I wish you the best for your first "Break a leg"!

I'm so happy to hear this, and proud of your work on what is really all our behalf (sane Americans) who feel mortified and ashamed of what happened two days ago, and terrified of what lies ahead for Ukraine.

The production sounds wonderful. If you tape it, and are allowed to show friends, sign me up.

It's truly a wonderful and important thing you're doing. It brings back the days when America had an active cultural department in US Information Agency, and actually sent us around the world as ambassadors.

I guess it's on all of us to do that now, and your work is an inspiring example in that direction.

Stay safe. And thank you for the first upbeat news I've had for weeks.

Little before 6pm, after rehearsal:

Just about to go have dinner with Larissa. She and her husband, Richard, are the foremost translators of Russian literature into English alive today. She, Richard and I have been translating Russian plays together for more than ten years; and Larissa and a friend of hers in Paris, where she lives, translated *Conversations in Tusculum* into Ukrainian last year for my production at Theater on Podil. She is a dear friend, and she arrived today in Kyiv.

We had a dress rehearsal which went beautifully; they all understood exactly what I am after, and it played beautifully. They were wonderful. I was moved.

At the end of the day, we got talking about crazy things they remember about the war: how my Vira happened to shave her legs on Feb. 23rd, day before the full-scale invasion, and then once it happened she decided she wasn't going to shave her legs again until the war was over. But by June 1st her husband was begging her to shave her legs, and so she did. That is something she remembers from those first months.

My Valentina made a joke. Because I have insisted that they do not wear any makeup in the play, she remembered that on the day of the full-scale invasion while Russia was pushing towards Kyiv, she took the time to put on makeup. But she doesn't today for my show.

We were very relaxed together after the dress.

My Vira explained how during the early air raids, she would take a shower and wash her hair, because she wanted to look nice in case something happened to her.

March 4th.
About 6:30am:

I woke up to this headline in The Times: "Trump administration suspends all military aid to Ukraine." The question is: does that include training, and intelligence? We'll see where that leads. Quite a time.

Today we have our first audience, an invited dress; it will be a full house of Mr. Benyuk's students, and at least one of my actors from *Tusculum*. After the show, I will speak to them, take their questions, for about a half an hour. That will be useful I hope—to me, maybe to them.

Oskar arrives on Saturday and I am still waiting to hear about Avignon.

Read this in The Economist: Saying that "something bigger is at stake, something Mr. Zelensky seemed to understand," and a quote from him: "If we lose a shipment or there is some delay that's something we've been through many times before, but if we lose our self-respect, that's not something you can ever compensate for, or restore."

About 8:30pm:

We had our invited dress; theater was packed, people sitting on the floor.

A good show; my young ladies were nervous, so they pushed in places, but for a first time in front of an audience they did very well.

I had a talkback after, and Benyuk said wonderful things about the importance of the play, and my being there. My Cicero from *Tusculum* came. He was crying after.

The students talked about how their story today, their lives today, was being told in the play. I asked what they thought or felt about an American coming to Kyiv and telling a story about a very important time in Ukrainian theater history. They said it was great to get such a perspective. One student said it was a perspective they needed to hear.

Tetiana, 'the head of the troupe' at the theater, was in tears; she said the play was about her life, and that so many of the stories the characters told had specific ties to her experiences.

I heard a lot of crying at the end of the show; and a lot of laughter throughout. I was proud of my ladies and they will even be better.

My Vira said she was having a problem with one of her speeches; and we talked. Later she wrote to me on Telegram explaining that this speech evokes her own life now; she said she hadn't wanted to tell me this, but—I had already guessed much of this—that both her mother and father are now in the Donbas, occupied by the Russians. Her grandmother is there; so her parents probably stayed or went back to take care of her. My Vira talks almost every day with her mother on the phone; she hasn't seen her father for two years and mother for a year and a half; and her grandmother for three. She was worried that I might think they were there for political reasons; and I answered, 'no, no, I understand that people are trapped.'

A moving day for me; on top of the terrible news from Washington about stopping arms delivery to Ukraine.

I'll go to bed now.

March 6th.
A little before 6:30am:

One air-raid-alert last night, it woke me up, but I stayed in bed.

The second invited dress yesterday went beautifully. I couldn't have been more pleased. Full house of actors, members of the theater's acting company, and that of course made my young actresses tense and nervous. I thought they handled themselves wonderfully.

Afterwards they had thought they had done terribly, and they were confused. I explained that this is the process with this work, because I am asking them not to push anything, not to 'act', and so they come away feeling that they are not doing anything. Also they don't have anything to hang onto and so at a loss. That's the process, the method of what I am trying to achieve, so as characters and actors they won't know what is going to happen in a scene, or even what they are going to say; it is very alive and present and they are dependent upon each other. We talked for a long time afterwards about this.

I know they got very positive feedback from friends and colleagues. One elderly actress wrote to everyone on Telegram:

> "I would like to thank everyone who made the play WHEN THE STORM OF EVIL DIES DOWN. I would like to talk about this, that is, about the very process of the birth of the script and the play... I saw a single organism that gradually captures me, and a story emerges in front of me, more than the story of the play, more than the story of Kurbas... And it's good that I don't find words, it's good that my inner space has become bigger, stronger, kinder... Thank you, Richard Nelson!"

Many people stopped me after to thank me and ask how as an American I could write this, such a Ukrainian play.

One woman said, in one breath two hours went by. People were crying at the end, of course, it is a dark and sad ending.

Today we'll come back, do a bit of rehearsal, then a dress just for photos and video, then a break, more rehearsal and then a show for the press at 6pm. The shows are always at six or earlier because of the curfew.

We're ready.

Tired, but satisfied.

Larissa saw it for the first time; she was full of praise, said it was a major play, about more than Ukraine.

Someone insisted that I had based this play on another play or story that was Ukrainian; how could I, an American, have written this from scratch?

The house manager of the theater held me and said that this was the story of her family; her grandmother lived during the time of the play, with four children, three daughters and a son. She told me that when one of the daughters starting saying, "Stalin, Stalin, or he's so good and interesting!" Her grandmother just said, "Wait, let's wait and see."

Went out to dinner with Larissa and Arman and was very pleased to discover that this is the first week of Lent, so the restaurant up the street has started to have its Lent menu, which is vegetarian. I had cauliflower steak which I very much like; it's only available during Lent, so I'm lucky.

The small theater we are in is legally supposed to have something like 55 seats, I have ignored this and added a few more; I said that we shouldn't tell anyone. When I said this to my actors, they said, "now you are a Ukrainian."

Yesterday, the theater copied me on an email they had just received from a good friend of mine, a wonderful actor, in America. They wanted to know if this was a scam.

> Hello from New York City,
>
> I am a friend of writer/director Richard Nelson's. I know Richard is currently working at your theatre. I would like to find a way to contribute some money in honor of his work at your theatre. But I am in America. I will try to find a way to do this through my bank. If you know of any other way to forward money, I would be grateful to find out. Do you have an international portal for support?
>
> Thank you for whatever assistance you can provide. And on behalf of many Americans I send you very best wishes to you and all at your theatre for continuing to shine the light of art in a terrible, dark time.

Now Trump seems to be slightly backpedalling, in his State of the Union Address, he did not even mention the embargo on weapons; instead saying he had received a letter from Zelensky, which he implied was an apology. According to those who have read the letter, it wasn't; Zelensky wrote only that he regretted the way the meeting went last Friday. Which I am sure he does as does much of the world. My guess is that this pause of arms deliveries may be a short one, let's pray so.

As the invited dress audience came into the theater yesterday, I stood in the aisle watching them, and I would say that probably 90% were women.

Reading this on Telegram, Times of Ukraine:

> "America cut a key Intel link for alerts at 2pm Kyiv... Ukraine is [no longer] receiving real time information of long-range strikes. 'Trump wanted a thank you,' said a source, 'we will be writing it on graves of dead Ukrainians.'"

About 9:30pm:

We had a photo dress which I didn't think went terribly well. I was disappointed in the way the theater organized things. A photo dress was my own idea—I choose to do a dress just for photographers or anyone videoing so that we can have a real performance in the evening uninterrupted by people taking photos, which is what happens normally in this theater. They combine both into one performance. The word got out that there was this photo dress, and seemingly they invited a bunch of other people to come, so we had maybe 30 people in the audience, which confused the event. It is supposed to be focused on the actors warming up, spending time on themselves, and not worrying about an audience, and experimenting. It was neither here nor there. Also as they had gotten very positive reactions from the previous night, they came out a little confident, and so forced and pushed. We had a long talk and lots of notes after.

They then gave a beautiful show.

There were press and whatever; it was a rather cold audience, with people sitting 'in judgement,' even though I've been told the press is very supportive of theater, given the situation. But we did very well and the actors were pleased. A moving show. Lots of tears that were real, spontaneous, and so earned.

My Syrus from *Tusculum* and his wife were there, and he seemed to like it a great deal.

I was reminded by Arman that my Cicero from *Tusculum*, who had seen the show two days before at an invited dress and had been deeply moved, had asked Arman to tell me that the play seems to give permission to cry. For Ukrainians now so much is being held in, he said, so much is about getting through the day; the play allowed one to open up and feel things, and cry. That is a wonderful compliment.

I read on Reuters that Trump is threatening to expel the 240,000 Ukrainian refugees from the war now living in the US. A very ugly turn, one obviously meant to stoke the fires under Zelensky's feet. Very mean. Beyond the pale.

March 7th.
About 7:50am:

The day of the first premiere.

A lot of alerts last night; I think it was a difficult night throughout Ukraine; one alert is still going on right now. I tried to sleep. Around 11:30 I woke up with a migraine which lasted almost two hours and was extremely painful. I think it is the dry heat, but I am mostly recovered now, though I feel like I have been through something. Off to breakfast, assuming it is open, because of the alert.

Just back from breakfast:

I ran into Larissa there. We had breakfast together and caught up; she had a busy day wandering through Kyiv yesterday; today she is seeing a friend, going to a porcelain museum, and stopping by the Bulgakov Museum before seeing my premiere at 6.

I have an interview at ten and rehearsal at two, between these I think I will take a walk, as it is suddenly spring in Kyiv, a beautiful day. I can finally wear my light jacket, the first time since I've been here. I'll go down the hill and do a little souvenir shopping for my family.

Larissa and I talked about Ukraine and what she has been reading. I'm not sure where she reads this—conspiracy theories about the close relations between Trump's children and Putin's children. I am not sure how true that is or what it means if it is true. But as always it's great to talk with her, she is full of life. She and her husband, Richard, will be part of a conference on Evil in Russian Literature and Philosophy in Cambridge UK this summer, so she has been thinking about the nature of evil in the books they have translated and other works. Of course all this completely blends in with the world as she sees it today. She spoke of a short story by Nikolai Leskov in which all the characters are 'good'; that is they try to do good. She called Leskov the genius of expressing 'goodness' and making that complex, human, and true. Once home I will reread this story, it is in their collection of Leskov stories.

I told her that I had heard from Arman that in France there are boycotts of American products.

My Bronia sent me this from someone writing on Instagram:

> "The chamber stage of the Theater on Podil. If this is déjà vu, it is expected and even desired. After Tuskul Talks, I was waiting for the next production by Richard Nelson.
>
> A play about Kurbas without Kurbas.
>
> A play about a past war that continues 100 years later.
>
> A fictional evening, fictional circumstances, fictional and real facts, phrases, memories.
>
> This never happened, but it's easy to imagine that such a conversation could have happened.
>
> I want more stories that are uncomplicated and emotionally true, want more of this kind of acting.
>
> "*When the Storm of Evil Dies Down*"
>
> Table, food, conversations."

About 12:30pm:

Just read that "Russia carried out a massive attack on Ukraine's energy structure, launching 70 missiles and 200 drones."

March 8th.
About 6:15am:

Just got up. Not sure if there were air raids; I slept right through them if there were.

I got a good night's sleep; less than I wanted, but fine.

Yesterday's first premiere was a triumph; I don't know what else to say. It was a beautiful performance; my ladies did well, incredibly focused, very moving. We had a good rehearsal beforehand, though they are a rather rowdy group; they are pretty excited about the show, about what they're doing, and proud.

I was called up on stage and asked to speak. I thanked everyone, especially my actresses, and I also spoke about my country. I said that right now, when my country was disappointing me and the whole world, that here I found a place where we could work together and make something—that 'here' being the theater.

My actresses said later to me, after the show, "you know we're trying to make a collection so we can buy a house for you and your wife in Kyiv." Very funny and of course moving. "And your wife can do whatever she wants here. She can plant a garden if she wants."

Before the show, Mr. Benyuk presented me with the published book of the script of the play in Ukrainian. It's an odd publication, because it's large in size, tall, wide, not like playscripts normally are. I don't think there is any real tradition of publishing playscripts in Ukraine. No one knew and no one really asked. A beautiful cover with the painting of Nijinska's *Fear*; it looks great. I'm very pleased that they were able to publish it. I will sign books later today to all my actresses and give out other copies to people around the production.

The reaction was very strong last night; Benyuk again spoke afterwards, praising me, talking about urging me to come back and write a play about the Ukrainian folk hero, Mazepa—something I will think about and research a bit to see if there is something for me there. He has the idea of a play about Mazepa with his mistresses, with his mistresses talking about him, I suppose, as the actresses in my play talk about Kurbas. I don't think I would want to go back and do that kind of thing again. Mazepa is a heroic figure in Ukraine; centuries ago he split Ukraine from Russia, making a pact with Sweden to create an Independent Ukraine. This fell apart after the battle of Poltava, and Mazepa died in exile. Pushkin wrote a long poem about him, so did Byron; Tchaikovsky wrote an opera, etc. Benyuk told me there was an American opera/play about him that was performed in the 19th century in New York. I will look that up..

A side note about Benyuk. He figures much more in this visit than last year's. Over the last ten weeks I have watched a number of movies on Ukrainian Netflix; two starred Benyuk. One was a beautiful film called *Mother of Apostles*, about a mother who goes looking for her son, a soldier and pilot, whose cargo plane crashed in the occupied territories. This was between the annexation of Crimea and before the full-scale invasion. She finds other crew members, meets Benyuk's character, and in the end finds out her son has died. It presents a very complex view of Ukraine and of the occupied Donbas. There was an element of the Wild West. Mr. Benyuk is a very big star here—stage, film, and TV. I also saw him in a TV series on Netflix. Yesterday he brought his son and future daughter-in-law to the show.

Today, Oskar arrives and I think he will see the show at 2. The Ukrainian Minister of Culture is coming. I'll sit him with Oskar; I believe he speaks English, and I heard he spent time in the Ukrainian consulate in San Francisco, where Oskar also lived while running a theater there.

Yesterday morning I had an hour-long television interview for Ukrainian TV, with a woman who had briefly interviewed me last year. She was extremely well-informed about Les Kurbas. I learned later that she is making a piece for BBC radio about Kurbas and so has been researching him. Her questions were smart and very thoughtful. She gave me a great compliment when she said she knew that all of the specific references in the play were true, but wasn't sure if the relationship between Valentina and Wanda, her mother-in-law and Les Kurbas' mother, was based on any facts. She asked if this had been my invention. I said, no, that this too came out of my research and I offered, when I got home, to send her my notes from where I found this story.

An extraordinary day. I felt that there was no place I would rather be right now than here.

An artistic director from another Kyiv theater was there last night; as he came in he stopped, and said hello to me, in English. He seemed to know me; I probably met him last spring. At the end of the play, he had a gift for me – a box of Ukrainian chocolates. He said, "Richard, everyone in Kyiv is talking about you. And you being here and doing this play." I think by "everyone in Kyiv" he meant, at most, people in the theater world here. But still...

6:50pm:

An eventful day.

We had a little bit of rehearsal; Oskar arrived; I briefly met the Minister of Culture. We started the show.

In the middle of the third scene the air-raid alert went off, and so we cleared the theater; I stayed with the actresses backstage. When the alert was finally over, I was told that my Lyuba wasn't feeling well, she was feeling faint. We held the show; the stage manager called for an ambulance. We held for a very long time. As we waited for the theater to figure out what to do (if we cancelled, they needed to find another date for the people seeing this show) I got up and just spoke to the patiently waiting audience and told them what was happening, adding that I could not make the decision to cancel.

The wait went on and on. My Lyuba's blood pressure was a little high, pulse a little high, but nothing much. Her blood sugar level was okay, but the person from the ambulance said she should go home and rest and not continue. She went home in a taxi.

In the meantime, while the theater continued to try to figure out another date for the show, I again began to speak to the audience, to tell them about the play, why I had written it, how I had written it, etc. When the cancellation was finally announced, some of the audience left, but most stayed and we talked a little bit more.

It was interesting; and I feel fine.

The Minister of Culture was calm about it; these people have gone through so much. As someone was saying, you come to the theater, you don't know if you're going to see the whole thing or not. You don't know. This is the way theater in Kyiv is today.

I learned that my Bronia's sister was in the audience, and I introduced myself to her. My Vira's husband was there too, and I introduced myself to him. My Bronia's husband came back, he had seen the show and photographed it a couple of days ago; he now brought with him their three-year-old daughter. I heard that my Valentina's father had also been in the audience; and so I said to her, "where's your father, come on, bring him back here—to the stage." So she went and got her father and mother.

I told them that there was going to be another show tomorrow, so they could come back. I figured we could find them seats or I could give up mine. My Valentina's father said, or almost mumbled, that he was in the military and only had a one-day pass.

I then realized he was going to miss his daughter's performance because of this situation. I didn't know what to say. I gathered everyone together—actresses, husbands, daughter, mother, father, and we took group pictures. We spent a nice time together, I think, like a kind of family. I adore these young women; and I think we made the most of a difficult situation.

The show had been magnificent up to the point of the air-raid alert. They know what they are doing; they are in good shape.

Oskar is interested in bringing this show to New York; possibly as early as this summer. That would be fantastic. We'll see, he's only seen half of it, but he read it on the train. I will set up a meeting between him and the managing director.

Oskar and I then had dinner at my favorite restaurant with the cauliflower steak—he had meat. We talked about a number of other projects. It was good to see him and I appreciate his being here. He came a long way for this. A very good and old friend.

A thwarted day; an unfinished day, but for some reason, I felt very relaxed about everything—that this is all part of doing a play in Kyiv right now.

Yesterday morning before everything that happened, I took a long walk with Larissa into the center of Kyiv. Went to a bookshop and I bought the English translation of Andrey Kurkov's *Ukraine Diaries*, which is the second installment of his diaries; the first, which I read on my way to Kyiv last spring, was set around the full-scale invasion. This book covers an earlier time, when Crimea was annexed by Russia and there were the Maidan protests. I look forward to reading it on the train tomorrow. I met Mr. Kurkov when he came to see my show last spring.

WEEK ELEVEN:

March 10th.
About 7:30am. My last day in Kyiv:

I catch an 8pm train to Warsaw tonight.

I'm sure throughout the day I will be adding thoughts from yesterday.

But first I just read of the death of Athol Fugard, a great playwright, a man I knew and greatly admired. He had a rich life, important career, influencing many people. A moral center who will be missed in these seemingly amoral times.

Yesterday I began the day with a walk down the hill to get some air; I ended the day with a terrible migraine that sent me to bed around 7pm. Between these two events, the day was thrilling.

I got to the theater at around 11:30; took measurements of the pieces of furniture and of the space we play in, so if we tour this show, we will be able to replace the furniture at the venues, as opposed to having it shipped from here. Replacing would be much cheaper, I'm sure.

I learned that my Lyuba would be coming in a bit late, a little before 1; she still felt exhausted. She asked if a line in the play could not be spoken—the line about Lyuba having fainted backstage a few weeks before. She just didn't want to be reminded of having felt faint, which was why she had to leave. I rewrote the line.

I met with my actresses who were in a wonderful mood, excited; I got the sense that this was an event today—that is, yesterday. My Lyuba arrived, she seemed quiet, subdued, anxious, but strong; we did a little bit of rehearsal; they prepared the stage, and then they gave me gifts and said wonderful things about working with me. They made little pins of the painting of Bronia's *Fear* dance; a T-shirt with the poster for Kurbas' 1920 *Macbeth* printed on the back—the poster that had inspired me to write this play; they gave me pencils with Kurbas' name, and a pad with the last line of the play, 'hope', in Ukrainian on the cover. Again, what they said about working on our show was deeply moving for me. That was just the beginning of a day of festivities.

My Cicero from *Tusculum* came with his wife to see it again; my Vira's husband came and as we had extra seats that are not supposed to be there we got him in; Oskar and Larissa were there. It was packed. Benyuk sat with my Olena's mother. I learned that my Olena came from the same small town as Benyuk, and that he knows her mother from there.

As the show began, it felt a little forced; I think everyone was worried about my Lyuba; so they were sort of 'protecting' her by pushing things, compensating for her. But she was strong; and by the second scene and certainly into the third scene, the play sort of 'kicked in' in a way that was unique and special.

Lyuba was a little different; she made an entrance that was too soon, but that was fine; and because she was different everyone was adjusting to that, and so everything was alive and fresh. An absolutely gorgeous performance. It just got better and better, deeper and deeper.

And there was no air-raid alert.

Then came the audience response. When the characters sing the song at the end, pounding the table and singing in defiance of what these characters will face in their lives, singing a silly Ukrainian song about dumplings, the audience joined in, first clapping, stomping, then singing along with the actresses.

When it was over and the actors were leaving the stage, the audience was on its feet in one second, before anyone had left the stage, and they were not just applauding, but literally cheering, and stomping. The actresses came back, they acknowledged me—and the audience let out a cheer—directed at me.

The actresses went off, and they were brought back. Benyuk then paused everything, came on stage, and gave another speech. Yulia came up next to me to translate in my ear. It was a speech about me, my being in Kyiv, in Ukraine, and how important this was to Ukrainian theater and to Ukraine; how I had, as a playwright, expressed things that had not been expressed before, and how necessary this was, to have me, from abroad, able to see their world, their lives, their complicated lives today. He told the audience that I would be coming back with a new play—in fact he said many new plays, maybe four!—one about Mazepa, the subject he has asked me now numerous times to write about. He called me on to the stage; hugged me, praised me; and the audience just started clapping, then pounding, then chanting—a kind of thank you to me.

I don't think I have ever been so welcomed in a theater before; and I felt I had done something, made something, created something that had brought together the theater, an audience, a world, a time, all entwined. All about now and here. I seem to have articulated something that people hadn't imagined could be articulated.

Later I was stopped on the street. I was thanked. As people were leaving the theater, many came to thank me and many wanted photos with me, saying how moving and how important this was.

I met the publisher of the book of the play; he was excited, proud, and pleased.

I went backstage to the dressing room and there was more celebration and joy. I could tell the actresses how wonderful they had been; tell my Lyuba about the courage she had shown, that she had brought a kind of fierceness to the play, because she was fighting her exhaustion and anxiety. The head of the company gave me two beautiful presents, an embroidered cloth for Cindy and a Ukrainian shirt for me. She too was in tears; she too said she loved me.

Earlier Larissa had brought me a gift from the Bulgakov Museum; the woman there sent gilded acorn Christmas ornaments. I'd given Larissa a copy of my *Diary of War and Theatre* for the museum's library. This was their gift back.

Afterwards we gathered in the little lobby of the theater; my Cicero was still in tears; via Yulia he gave us extraordinary praise, again and again saying how what we had done mattered so much, was so badly needed, and how significant this play is for Ukraine right now. He kept saying, in English, "Richard, why aren't you President?"

I handed out copies of the published play to the lighting designers, sound designer, stage managers. I signed all their copies. Earlier in the day I had signed copies to all my actresses. I had told them I would sign the same to all: the name of their character, my love, and my name. As they all share a dressing room I didn't want them to read what I might write about each of the others.

There was food at this little party; they knew I am vegetarian so they made a large plate just for me—fruit, vegetables, cheese, etc. They said, "this was made for Richard."

Then my actresses, in preface to a toast, spoke one after the other about me, the experience they had, its importance to them, and how it has changed the way they work and even their lives. Two of them said it was like having an incredible "grandfather" guiding them. I caught Oskar's eye, he was smiling. "Grandfather." I almost said, "I had seen myself as your older brother." But I didn't. Each spoke beautifully.

Then I spoke back, addressing them, and telling them how important it had been for me that they allowed themselves to share their experiences, their losses, fears, worries, in this process; such experiences had deepened the play and production. How open they were able to be with me, and how much I appreciated that.

I repeat again that when I sent the play to Benyuk, I had said it was a play about a group of young women putting on a play in the middle of a war, to be performed by a group of young women putting on this play in the middle of a war. And how those two things would entwine and become the heart of my ambition for this venture. And that is what we have achieved.

Oskar and I left to return to the hotel so I could drop off my knapsack and the various presents I'd received, including yet another from my actresses: a poster—photoshopped to show my actresses surrounding Les Kurbas, and now with me added as well.

We returned to meet Arman and Yulia in front of the theater, and there were all my actresses waiting to wave goodbye. I joked, referencing the play, I started to take off my coat to give it to them, as happened to the characters with the Ukrainian/Canadians who visited Kurbas and his company, offering them a theater in Canada, but wanting them to perform 'old fashioned' Ukrainian theater. Kurbas had turned them down; as they departed one of the actresses admired one of the Canadians' coats; she immediately took it off and gave it to the actress. After that, all the other actresses admired the Canadian's coats, but no more were given out.

Arman went off with friends so Yulia, Oskar, and I went down the hill to the Georgian restaurant, which was full; we tried a Crimean restaurant that had a 30-minute wait, so we went back up the hill to the restaurant I have been to now so many times, and where everyone knows me. The women at the next table had seen the show and they wanted to thank me, saying I had written something that felt so true to them, about themselves, about women.

There I started to have the migraine, so I just sort of faded away. I quietly had my dinner and let Oskar and Yulia talk, which was great, Oskar getting to know Yulia and from her, learning a lot about Ukraine today. I excused myself, quickly went back to the hotel; wrote Cindy that all went well, but couldn't talk, and went to bed.

That was yesterday.

5:45pm:

I will be picked up by the managing director in about an hour and fifteen minutes to be taken to the train station.

A slow day; I am realizing just how tired I am, and finding that if I take my eye drops any sense of a headache coming seems to go away, so I think I am just dehydrated with dry eyes, which then builds up into a headache.

I packed everything, including my winter coat that I arrived in; so I can wear my spring jacket.

I had a meeting with the managing director and Oskar, with Yulia translating. Oskar is interested in bringing the production to New York at the Public Theater for a short run, perhaps as early as August. He wants to do another screening of my film/video of my Kyiv production *Conversations in Tusculum* [the Public also screened it last November], this time at the Delacorte, the huge 3,000 seat outdoor theater in Central Park. Oskar is looking for ways to make a statement of support for Ukraine in this troubled time. He thinks this could be a good way of doing so; the screening and bringing over this production at the same time. I suggested we do the play in the smallest theater, The Shiva, which has 100 seats.

We went through the details of the finances; Theater on Podil does not want to get any money from the Public, which surprised Oskar, so the costs would only be the train tickets, airfare, hotel, per diems, and visas. The Public pays for operators, rehearsal, etc. It would not be an expensive show to tour. I look forward to seeing what Oskar can do over the next couple of weeks.

I took a stroll down to have lunch by myself at the Crimean restaurant; came back up the hill while looking for things to buy my family. I bought a few hats with the trident symbol of the Ukrainian army, a painted hairbrush for my granddaughter, earrings for one daughter, a Ukrainian flag patch for her as well, per her request. She wants to put it in the window of her home in Rhode Island.

Bought some food for the trip: yogurt, apple juice, nuts, pretzels. They sell nothing on the train but coffee.

Came back and repacked a bit, began to read Andrey Kurkov's book, *Ukraine Diaries*, about the Maidan Revolution in 2013-2014.

Called Cindy; had a quick salad with Larissa in the hotel restaurant. She unfortunately seems to have gotten a cold, or maybe it's allergies; she has been running around a lot while here and maybe wore herself out.

I now wait to get on the train.

From Instagram:

> "I attended the premiere of *When the Storm of Evil Dies Down* on March 7, and I highly recommend it.... The play is performed on a small stage, which creates a special intimacy.
>
> It's as if you're sitting with the actresses in their kitchen, discussing the *Macbeth* play they just performed with Les Kurbas. The girls were incredible in their roles: no falsity, sincere emotions, and a special vibe of female conversation between them.

The play was staged by an American director who attended the premiere in person and sincerely apologized for the current leaders of his country."

I now wait to start my journey home.

8:30 pm.
On the train, just leaving Kyiv:

The managing director drove us to the station; Larissa, Oskar, Arman, and myself. Oskar and Arman are on the part of the train that separates at the border; they will then get off and wait for another train to take them on to Warsaw. Larissa and I stay on the train while its tracks are fitted for the European gauge, all the way to Warsaw.

I learned on the short drive that my actresses have been told of the possibility of going to New York, and that they are, of course, incredibly excited.

We waited in a very comfortable lounge at the train station, and then walked down along the platform to the front of the train to carriage #3, where I was surprised and moved to find my Vira and my Olena waiting for me, holding up a sign saying, "We love you, Richard!" And holding up a phone with my other actresses there live to also say goodbye. A beautiful surprise. They had packed a bag of food for me—"all vegan," my Vira said—nuts, juices, apple sauce, vegetable chips.

As I got on the train, they followed me from outside until I got to my compartment; and they stood at the window waving, and pointing to their sign.

March 11th.
A little after 11am, Polish time:

I am still on the train, it is an hour and half late. Fortunately my flight isn't until 4:40, and the airport is only about 20 minutes away from the Warsaw train station.

I read on the news that Ukraine had launched its largest drone attack against Russia since the start of the full-scale invasion; even hitting Moscow. Obviously, they wish to make a point that, unlike what Trump says, Ukraine does have a few cards to play.

Today negotiators from Ukraine and the UK meet in Saudi Arabia to begin to discuss a ceasefire.

Slept pretty well, except for the almost four hours we were at the border, where one is interrupted by customs agents, first from Ukraine (soldiers) and then from Poland, and by the pounding and jerking of the changing of the gauge of the train wheels.

I keep fighting off little headaches, but I think that's because I'm just tired.

***

March 12th.
About 7:30am:

Back in Rhinebeck, got home a little before midnight (6am Kyiv time); fairly easy trip, customs at Newark Airport was empty, my bag was waiting for me, the person picking me up was right there. No traffic; and I slept in the car most of the way. Just really long.

Woke up to the news that Ukraine has agreed to a ceasefire, and the US has agreed to continue to supply it with weapons and intelligence. Now the ball is in Russia's court, they say.

Just read an email from my friend R. Once again, as always. he expresses his fears and anxieties in very strong terms; saying what a disaster we have in our country, and that we stand at the edge of a cliff.

These are dark times.

One thing I learned from Ukraine is that there are good, smart, surviving people who live or who have lived under very corrupt governments. You look around the world and you see that that is the case for most people. We Americans have been protected, comforted, maybe even spoiled. We have been proud of our country, proud of our government—in most cases at most times—and what it has stood for. Of course there have been great setbacks—Vietnam, Iraq—but we have had it pretty easy. We have felt ourselves somehow special. One of the truths that we now may be facing is that we may not be so special after all.

Reviews of 'When the Hurlyburly's Done' at the Theatre on Podil, Kyiv, Ukraine

[all translations via DeepL]

From Instagram:

"A performance where it was uncomfortable to cough, because you were a step away from the actors and, it seemed, if you made any sound, they would turn to you and start a conversation with you. Or they would sit you down at the table next to me and ask me how I was doing, ask me to help peel the potatoes, make the pies, or heat up the dumplings... As for the dumplings: I wanted them from the first minute of the performance, as soon as they were put on the table, until the last (a warning to the audience from the theater "don't come hungry"). And what an unexpected ending with the "dumplings" (I won't spoil it)... So yes, the performance resembles a chatter in the kitchen in women's company. Not gossip and slander. But such sincere, honest, heartfelt, painful, girlish ones... Where everyone cares about each other, where each friend is important, unique, special. And since most of them are actresses (from the Les Kurbas Theater), a rehearsal of the play (*Macbeth*) will be a bonus... I wonder how the American Richard Nelson managed to process the history of our Ukrainian artists in such a short time, to present them in such a special way... It is worth adding about the good translation by Yulia Sosnovska. In short, the play is on the list of favorites."

Hanna Veselovska, Ukrainian theatre critic:

"In the middle of the large room, young women sit at a table. They are peeling potatoes, sorting through kitchen utensils, making dumplings, sometimes singing and talking, talking, talking. In the corners and in the makeshift amphitheater, the audience hides, peering over their backs, looking at the flour and dough as if to check its taste. This is the second time that American director Richard Nelson has tried this tactile way of creating performances at the Kyiv Theater on Podil. At first, he staged his own play *Conversations in Tusculum* about ancient Rome in 46 B.C. in the chamber hall named after Igor Slavinsky. And recently he staged another of his texts, *When the Hurlyburly's Done*, about Ukraine in 1920.

Many believe that there is no connection between the historical events chosen by Richard Nelson. In one case, rebels conspire in a Roman villa, and in the other, Les Kurbas's traveling theater troupe Kyidramte (a contemporary abbreviation of the full name of the Kyiv Drama Theater) finds itself at the center of a Brownian movement through Ukrainian lands by the armies of the UPR and Pilsudski, red, white, and green. But the visual similarities between these performances are obvious: all the events are organized around tables and they do not spill over into the home space. Also, in both plays, Kyiv actors become full-fledged carriers of the characters' destinies, psychology, and habits, as if they dive into someone else's body, appropriating the thoughts and feelings of distant and unfamiliar people.

At the Roman table, political affairs are discussed by historical figures Brutus (Roman Khalaimov) and Cassius (Artem Atamaniuk), who are occasionally joined by Cicero (Serhii Boyko) and visited by women —Brutus' wife and mother, Portia (Maria Demenko) and Servilia (Maria Rudkovska). They drink wine and water in warmth and luxury, argue and fail to find common solutions. At the Ukrainian table are the media faces of future stars of the world and Ukrainian stage: Bronislava Nijinska (Natalka Kobizka), Lyubov Hackenbusch (Maria Demenko), Valentina Christyakova (Katerina Chikina), and lesser-known actresses Vira Onatska (Yulia Brusentseva), Olena Galitsynsak (Maria Kos), and the fictional Maria (Olena Korzeniuk). Feeling the cold of the coming autumn, the women sip herbal tea and moonshine, discuss children, food, and men.

It seems that the American Richard Nelson, by combining Rome and Ukraine, unintentionally and technically approached the events in one way, through the psychological portraits of their participants. He encouraged each performer to maximize the character's individuality, convinced them to move away from emotional generalities, sketches, and to find something in their eyes, movements, or voices to reproduce the inner confusion of the participants in long conversations. So, if you put them together at the same table, you get a large group of anxious people who are desperate, hiding fear from themselves and afraid to look into the future. Both of them are at the moment of breaking their own destinies, the most important choice in life, after which it's either this way or not at all.

In both performances, the director's compulsion to "immerse oneself in time and fate" worked, and the small theater space absorbed and mixed distant times, epochs, plots, and events. But it is not known what is more difficult to imagine—Brutus without Brutus' pose, Cicero without speeches, or women from Les Kurbas' circle discussing the master behind his back, doubting him, hesitating in their rightness. Recognizable from photographs from educational websites, the characters here are extremely ordinary, like women frightened by the war who are constantly inventing something to save their children and themselves. Unlike *Conversations in Tusculum*, where meetings and conversations last for months and the characters gradually change psychologically, in *When the Hurlyburly's Done* the events are compressed into one evening, during which the characters are confirmed in their own decisions.

The dinner in a Ukrainian house is hosted by the practical and reserved Lyubov Hackenbusch, who is more experienced than most, and will be a three-time performer of Lady Macbeth on various Ukrainian stages. Despite the storm, she is confident in herself, even in her future, as she is about to marry Vasya, an actor and director named Vasyl Vasylko, who will become a well-known figure in the Ukrainian theater of the twentieth century. No less remarkable is the choreographer Bronislava Nijinska, a purposeful, determined, courageous woman who seems to foresee her unique artistic mission. And the youngest member of this women's company is Les Kurbas's young wife, Valentina Christyakova, who is impetuous, tense, and nervous. The actresses of the Podil Theater played all the roles with exceptional delicacy and precision, so that the usual photographic representations of famous Ukrainian artists are leveled, and the references of contemporaries to Hackenbusch's erotomania or Christyakova's intransigence and pride seem like fantasies.

Another surprise from an intellectual from another continent, Richard Nelson: by proposing an intimate 'Peeping Tom' theater, he provoked us, the moderns, to take a closer look at our own past, which, as in the past, is already being covered by an opportunistic veil. The most controversial personality of the 1920s is Les Kurbas, who is not on stage, but is always talked about, trying to understand his intentions and actions, not artistic but political. They say that Kurbas is negotiating a deal with the Reds, so that Kydramte will receive protection and financial support from the Bolsheviks. In contrast, they tell horror stories about the shooting of Jews, recall funny encounters, arrests of friends, and love stories.

And everything that is not talked about comes down to the play *Macbeth*, which has just been performed and will most likely be performed again tomorrow for the Red Army. So the rehearsal of the witch scene from Shakespeare's tragedy is the culmination of a performance that does not follow the usual course of events, but is full of excesses and intrigue. Through the sharp, crippling movements of magical creatures that seem to deform the world, the tragedy of Kurbas's final choice is revealed better than any words. And the little-known actress Vira Onatska is the most expressive in this witch dance, which choreographer Charlotte Bydwell created, apparently inspired by Bronislava Nizhynska's recordings and drawings, her references to the Kyiv School of Movement, and her collaboration with avant-garde artists Oleksandra Ekster and Vadym Meller.

This role was given to Yulia Brusentseva, who, as Vera, balances between different moods and life positions throughout the long dinner, consoling and reassuring some, explaining the good intentions of others, in short, existing between the drops, relying on common sense. But the fact that Vira Onatska's character in the play seems to lack confidence and understanding of the moment is transformed by the optics of the theater into the character's convincingness: she does not invent the future, but anticipates its tragedy. Therefore, the actress in this role or the role in the actress Yulia Brusentseva exist optimistically doomed, knowing that *Macbeth* is a trap for the Red Army soldiers in 1920 in the village between Uman and Bila Tserkva, but the choice is inevitable.

Later, Vira Onatska would found the Berezil artistic association, and, inspired by Kurbas's ideas, she would organize a propaganda theater workshop—the Berezil branch in Boryspil. Then she would be arrested and imprisoned. Thus, among all the women at the table, two of whom would leave Ukraine and two of whom would become People's Artists, Vira Onatska would go through the most exemplary path of the 1920s—from enthusiastic dreaming to despair. For her, the "Hurlyburly" will never subside, and the memories of Kurbas, his *Macbeth*, and the cold September evenings between Uman and Bila Tserkva will likely remain with her until her last days."

From Facebook:

"The performance is beautiful. Sincere, without unnecessary pathos or boasting. Richard is an American with a Ukrainian soul. We must feel so deeply our tragedy of the losses of that time and our losses today. Richard must be so sincerely fascinated by our Genius to write a play about him. Thank you!!!"

From Theater Magazine:

Six characters and an American in love

"After the success of last year's *Conversations in Tusculum*, Richard Nelson staged his second play, *When The Hurlyburly's Done*, at the Kyiv Theater on Podil. The premiere took place on March 7, 8, 9.

Richard seems to have fallen in love. When this happens, a man, even if he is an American, wants to know the history of the object of his love. Because it's not enough for him to have what he has, he wants to be with his love not only now, but also once before. The play and the performance seem to be based on an eternally sacramental question: "How did I live while you were gone? How did you live while I was gone?"

So, Richard Nelson wrote a play about six actresses who, in the fall of 1920, somewhere in a village near Bila Tserkva, performed Kurbas's *Macbeth* and sat down to dinner. It's night outside, and every street has its own *Macbeth*, and there is a war going on that is still going on in Ukraine to this day.

Nelson looks at all this with an anxious and fascinated look.

Accidentally or not, there are six characters here, just like Pirandello in *Six Characters in Search of an Author*. By the way, *Six Characters...* was staged twice in this theater. Pirandello's and Nelson's plays have something in common, namely the principle of "theater as life and life as theater."

Before the beginning, the actors spread a rug on the floor as an illustration of the statement about what theater is. This seems to be the director's favorite ritual. It was the same in *Conversation in Tusculum.*

It's a late dinner, where the actresses just sit at the table, eating slowly, listening to the shots fired outside, talking about their children and husbands, gossiping a little or wondering where to escape from this war, to Prague, Vienna, or further. They recall the first scene with the witches in the recently performed *Macbeth*. And that evil spirits in the person of the Bolshevik commissar may have already tempted Les Kurbas to serve the devil.

Most of the characters in the play have real-life prototypes related to Kurbas. His wife Valentina Christyakova is played by Katerina Chikina. Maria Demenko plays Lyubov Hackenbusch, Natalka Kobytska plays Bronislava Nijinska, and Yulia Brusentseva plays Vira Onatska. Lesser-known characters are played by Maria Kos (Olena Galitsynsak) and Olena Korzeniuk (Maria). However, in portraiture, they all look like no one but themselves. In the end, the play is not really about Kurbas's theater or even about 1920, but about what happened or is happening a hundred years ago or now to people who gather around the same evening table in the middle of a war.

This is a play about what we lose every night or are afraid of losing."

From Ostap Theater, Kateryna Kirsenko:

When The Hurlyburly's Done... but no, it won't.

"Let's be honest—we couldn't write this review for two months. And it's not that we have any excuse. We just couldn't find the words. You literally can't describe what you feel, and you leave the theater in a daze, with round and teary eyes.

The performance is paralyzing. And we're not afraid to use big words —this is one of the plays that has emotionally affected us the most recently.

The play *When The Hurlyburly's Done* is by American playwright and director Richard Nelson. Another of his works, *Conversations in Tusculum*, is also part of the theater's repertoire.

The director invites us back to 1920, when Les Kurbas, the founder of the Berezil Theater, leaves Kyiv for the countryside with his troupe.

There they put on performances, exchanging tickets for food.

While Kurbas and most of the troupe attend a local theater performance staged in their honor, six young women—four actresses, a pianist, and a dancer—stay with their children. But instead of the expected story about a great director, we find ourselves in a confined space where these six women are trying to keep a sense of home, at least for a moment.

Throughout the evening, we watch them talking, cooking dinner, acting out scenes, gossiping, laughing, and dancing. Nothing much seems to be happening, and yet everything is happening. Their monologues sound like diaries, and the silence between their lines is a reminder of a future that does not belong to them. We know that this "storm of evil" will not subside, that many will be repressed, sent to camps or shot. But they do not know this yet.

This is already very sad, but something else touched us..

A Few Lines from the Play:

"—Dream of what? —Obtaining abroad. —Well, what should I do there?"

"They were looking for Ukraine, which they left many years ago. They just wanted to see it."

"It's too late to leave. I feel like I'm falling."

"What are we all waiting for? What are we hoping for? It's all wrong. It just feels so empty."

"Wouldn't it be nice to just talk about everyday life. Together."

There should be a meme here that says "we've been there before," but it makes me want to cry more than laugh. Didn't we say these phrases at the beginning of the full-scale invasion after February 24, 2022? Only the words "Bolsheviks" and "Red Army" bring the viewer back to the idea that we are talking about the twenties, not about the present day Ukrainians.

From the very first minutes, it seems that there is no audience in the theater, and the actors are not acting. As if you were just allowed to spy on the everyday life of the characters. They are cooking real food (fried potatoes), gossiping, solving everyday problems. The actors are not afraid to speak with their backs to the viewer, take off their socks, or become uncomfortable for the camera.

The space is almost empty, which allows you to focus on emotions without being distracted by the outside. The audience seats are located around the stage, and each time you can watch this 'life' from a different angle.

The play highlights important aspects such as preserving dignity and the ability to make choices even when these choices seem meaningless or hopeless.

The deepest conflicts unfold in personal relationships, particularly between creative people who often have different views on how to deal with political and social challenges. It is through these conflicts, the search for answers to questions about morality and honor, that the play reaches its peak of emotional intensity.

Just like the characters in the play, Ukrainians today face enormous challenges that force them to rethink their moral guidelines, their habits and beliefs. The play reminds us of how important it is to preserve humanity even in the most difficult times, not to lose ourselves in the political and social chaos.

One hundred years have passed, and people still gather around the table amidst the roar of war to remember that they are alive, that they can still be together, even when the world is cracking around them."

APPENDIX:

'When The Hurlyburly's Done' at The Theater on Podil Kyiv, Ukraine

Translated into Ukrainian by Yulia Sosnovska

Vira	**Yulia Brusentseva**
Valentina	**Katerina Chikina**
Lyubov	**Maria Demenko**
Bronia	**Natalka Kobytska**
Maria	**Olena Korzeniuk**
Olena	**Maria Kos**
Director	**Richard Nelson**
Choreographer	**Charlotte Bydwell**
Set and Costume & Designer	**Maria Pogrebnyak**
Lighting Designer	**Sergey Nevgodovsky**
Sound Designer	**Sergey Shevchenko**
Music	**Timur Polyanskiy**
Assistant Director	**Arman Saribekyan**
Stage Managers	**Vladslav Tsekhmeistruk** **Milada Samoilova**
Translators	**Yulia Sosnovska** **Milada Samoilova**

For Theatre on Podil

Artistic Director	**Bohdan Benyuk**
Managing Director	**Yevhen Syvnov**
Deputy Director	**Nataliia Chernenko**
Main Artist	**Mariia Pohrebniak**
Head of the Troupe	**Tetiana Antonova**
Production Manager	**Alla Miarkovska**
Head of Drama Department	**Oksana Prybish**
Coffee and lunch	**Yana Muzyra**

PHOTOGRAPHS:

Sources:

* Photos by Theater on Podil Press Department

** Photo by Rustam Himadiiev

\+ Photos by Lenka Kirchenko-Povolotska

All others by the author.

ACKNOWLEDGEMENTS:

I need to thank everyone at the Theater on Podil, Kyiv: Bohdan Benyuk, the Artistic Director, for inviting me back to direct, for responding so well to the play when it was sent, and for his generous public praise for the production; Yevhen Syvnov, the Managing Director, and his Deputy, Nataliia Chernenko, for shepherding me around Kyiv; Tetiana Antonova, the Head of the Troupe, for her constant encouragement; and to the entire troupe who always made me feel welcome.

I could not have written this play without the active help, both in researching and producing the play, of Oksana Prybish. She fed me books to read, answered my queries, encouraged and supported me throughout, only pausing, briefly, to give birth to Matthew. This play owes her a great deal.

Yulia Sosnovaka, by every account, created a gorgeous, faithful, and loving translation of the play. She also sat at my side throughout rehearsals, translating with grace, humor, incredible speed, and intelligence. A gifted actress herself, she was a gift to both playwright and director. Arman Saribekyan, my dear friend and brilliant actor from Paris, travelled a long way to support this production; daily, he infused the rehearsals with his ever-present warmth and insights.

I thank my designers, Mariia Pohrebniak, Sergey Nevgadovsky, Sergey Shevchenko, and my stage manager Vlad Tsekhmiestruk; we are now a well-oiled team.

I want to thank with all my heart my six beautiful actresses who put on a play, for sharing their lives, for trusting me, and for teaching me so much. They are the reason for this book.

I should thank the entire staff, especially the restaurant waiters, of the Vozdvyzhensky Hotel, who looked after with care and good humor.

I must thank Susie Sainsbury for her generosity which made all this possible, as well as the Marguit Greiser Fund and its head, Oskar Eustis, and Susan Hilferty.

My friend of 40 years, Colin Chambers, helped edit this book with his usual care and thoughtfulness, and as always I owe him a great deal. And I thank Lucy George, the publisher, for her continued support and passion for this book; I thank my very close friend Larissa Volokhonsky for traveling to Kyiv when she was needed.

I thank Avery and Jocelyn, as I know that my journeys to Kyiv are never easy for them. And finally I thank Cynthia for accepting the risks of my journey, being the first reader of my plays, for helping to edit all my work including this book, for the pleasure she takes in these adventures, and for her love.

Also from Wordville by Richard Nelson

In the midst of war, spending nine weeks directing his play, *Conversations in Tusculum*, in Kyiv, Ukraine, American playwright and director Richard Nelson kept a diary. Here the mundane, the artistic, and the ongoing war entwine in a visceral account of making theatre in a different world at a time and a place where it has come to have a very special meaning.

A profoundly moving, exceptional, essential story, full of humor, self-questioning, confusions, doubts, fears, heartbreak, and joy, set in the middle of a beautiful, magical city under attack.

A DIARY OF WAR & THEATRE

Making Theatre in Kyiv, Spring 2024

Richard Nelson

Paperback
ISBN 9781399991964
Published 15th October 2024

"In this deeply stirring chronicle of making theater in a time of war, Richard Nelson deploys the same sensibility that shapes his plays, moving from curiosity to empathy to invaluable insight."
—**Ben Brantley**

Wordville

www.ingramcontent.com/pod-product-compliance
Lightning Source LLC
Chambersburg PA
CBHW060329260626
47160CB00007B/2737